RISE & SHINE

SOL Prep
Grade 3
Reading Comprehension
with Extra Writing Practice

by Jonathan D. Kantrowitz

Edited by Sarah M.W. Espano and Patricia F. Braccio

Item Code RAS 2005 • Copyright © 2009 Queue, Inc.

Queue, Inc. • 80 Hathaway Drive, Stratford, CT 06615
(800) 232-2224 • Fax: (800) 775-2729 • www.qworkbooks.com

Table of Contents

To the Students

In this reading comprehension workbook, you will read many fiction and nonfiction passages, as well as some poetry. You will then answer multiple-choice and open-ended questions about what you have read.

As you read and answer the questions, please remember:

- You may refer back to the text as often as you like.

- Read each question very carefully and choose the **best** answer.

- Indicate the correct multiple-choice answers directly in this workbook. Circle or underline the correct answer.

- Write your open-ended responses directly on the lines provided. If you need more space, use a separate piece of paper to complete your answer.

Here are some guidelines to remember when writing your open-ended answers:

- Organize your ideas and express them clearly.

- Correctly organize and separate your paragraphs.

- Support your ideas with examples when necessary.

- Make your writing interesting and enjoyable to read.

- Check your spelling and use of grammar and punctuation.

- Your answers should be accurate and complete.

Tips for Answering Multiple-Choice Questions

Multiple-choice questions have a stem, which is a question or incomplete sentence, followed by four answer choices. You should select only one answer choice. The following are some tips to help you correctly answer multiple-choice questions on the Grade 3 SOL Reading Assessment:

- Read the question carefully to make sure you understand what it is asking.

- Try to come up with an answer in your head before reading the answer choices. If you know the answer to a question, it will be much easier for you to choose the right answer choice. This way, the answer choices won't throw you off track.

- Read and consider all answer choices. Don't mark your answer until you have read all of the choices.

- Eliminate answer choices that you know to be incorrect.

- Don't be afraid to go back and reread the passage or parts of the passage to help you choose the right answer.

- If a question has a choice that says "all of the above" and you see at least two answers that seem to be correct, "all of the above" is probably the right answer.

- A positive answer is more likely to be true than a negative answer (an answer with *not* in it).

- Don't keep changing your answer. Most often, your first choice is the right one.

- Often—but not always—the correct answer is the longest or most detailed answer.

- Answer questions that you are sure of first. If a question seems really hard, skip it and then come back to it later.

- On the SOL Reading Assessment, there is no penalty for guessing. Try to answer all of the questions. If you really can't figure out the answer to a question, take the best guess you can.

- Be sure to completely fill in the answer bubbles in your test book or answer document. Don't make any stray marks around the answer spaces.

- Notice that odd-numbered questions have answer choices labeled A, B, C, D, and even-numbered questions are labeled F, G, H, and J. Be sure to fill in the bubble for the correct question.

- If you decide to change your answer to a question, make sure you erase your first answer completely.

- Fill in only one answer to a question.

A FURRY FRIEND

1. Myron looked into each cage at the animal shelter. He carefully watched each puppy for a few minutes.

2. "How about this cute little guy?" asked his older sister, Lydia. She pointed to a beautiful puppy with shiny black fur and big brown eyes. Myron held out his hand toward the puppy. The puppy sniffed his hand a few times and then walked to the back of his cage. The puppy did not seem very interested in Myron.

3. "No, he's not right," said Myron, his voice full of <u>disappointment</u>.

4. Myron moved to the next cage and then the next one. All of the puppies looked nice, but Myron wanted a puppy that would be his best friend. None of the puppies were excited to meet him. They didn't seem like they'd be very pleasant playmates.

5. "Myron, you better hurry up," Lydia said and tugged on his sleeve. "The shelter's going to close soon."

6. Myron kept looking. After a few more minutes, he pointed to a cage. "This one," he said.

7. Lydia looked where Myron was pointing. Inside the cage sat a puppy with shaggy gray fur. One of his ears stood straight up and the other flopped over.

8. "Are you sure you want this one?" asked Lydia. "He's not very pretty."

9. "I don't care what he looks like," said Myron. "I can tell by his eyes that he wants to be my friend. That's all that matters." As if the puppy understood, he wagged his tail playfully. He couldn't wait to get out of his cage and give Myron a big dog hug.

10. Lydia smiled. "We'll take this one," she said to the worker behind the counter.

1

1 This story is mostly about —

(A) choosing a pet
B taking care of dogs
C spending time with family
D learning about animals

When you think about the story you just read, what do you remember most? What do you think the story is mostly about? It might be about choosing a pet (answer choice **A**). In the story, Myron looks at some dogs and tries to pick one to have as a pet. This seems like the right choice, but be sure to read the others to make sure. Answer choice **B** is probably not the best. The story doesn't tell you much about caring for dogs. Myron does talk with his sister, Lydia, in the story. He is spending time with someone in his family (answer choice **C**), but that's probably not the most important idea in the story. Also, the story does not tell you much about animals (answer choice **D**). Answer choice **A** is best.

2 Would you have chosen the puppy Myron chose? Why or why not?

I would not want the puppy she chose because he did not seem like a normal dog. He also seemed down.

You have to write out your answer to this question. You might write an answer like this:

I would definitely have chosen the same puppy that Myron chose. What good is a dog that doesn't want to be your best friend? I also think that beauty is on the inside. Even if a dog isn't pretty, it doesn't matter. What matters is that you like the dog and it likes you.

3 **In paragraph 3, what does the word <u>disappointment</u> mean?**

   A excitement
   B sadness
   C silliness
   D anger

Read the sentence with "disappointment" in it carefully. You can find it easily by looking for the underlined word in the story. This sentence tells about Myron when he sees a dog he doesn't want for a pet. Answer choice **A** is *excitement*. But when Myron sees this dog, he isn't excited. He probably feels a little sad (answer choice **B**). He has no reason to feel silly (answer choice **C**) or to be angry (answer choice **D**). Answer choice **B**, *sadness*, is the best choice.

4 **Myron chooses the shaggy gray puppy because —**

   F he thinks the puppy looks pretty
   G he thinks Lydia will like the puppy
   H he thinks the puppy will be easy to train
   J he thinks the puppy will be his friend

Think about the story you just read. Why does Myron pick the last puppy, the shaggy gray one? That puppy is less pretty than the other dogs in the shelter, so answer choice **F** isn't right. Myron isn't worried about whether or not Lydia likes the dog, so answer choice **G** isn't best either. The puppy doesn't seem like it will be more or less easy to train, as stated in answer choice **H**. Myron chooses the dog because he feels the dog will be a good friend for him. Answer choice **J** is correct.

5   Read these sentences from the story.

> After a few more minutes, he pointed to a cage. "This <u>one</u>," he said.

Which one of these sounds the same as the underlined word?

A oil
B won
C on
D warn

This question asks you to find a homophone for the underlined word. A homophone is a word that sounds just like another word, but is spelled differently and has a different meaning. Look at the underlined word *one*. Now look at the answer choices. Answer choice **A**, *oil*, begins with an *o*, but it does not sound like the word *one*. Answer choice **B**, *won*, sounds just like the word *one*. This is probably the correct answer. Answer choice **C** also begins with an *o*, but *on* does not sound like *one*. *Warn*, answer choice **D**, does not sound the same as the word *one*. Answer choice **B** is the correct answer. *Won* and *one* are homophones.

6   Myron can BEST be described as —

F mean
G lonely
H angry
J tired

What do you think about Myron? What kind of a boy is he? He isn't mean to anyone in the story, so answer choice **F** isn't right. Myron wants the dog to be his best friend – a playmate; answer choice **G** is a good answer. He must not have a good friend or playmate at home. Myron isn't angry about anything (answer choice **H**) or tired (answer choice **J**). Answer choice **G**, "lonely," best describes Myron.

7 **Look at this picture.**

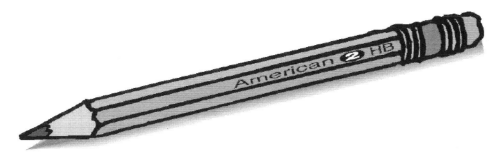

Which word from the story begins with the same sound?

A friend
B sister
C puppy
D cage

This question asks you to use what you know about language and word sounds. The picture shows a pencil. What other word from the story begins with a *p* sound? *Friend* (answer choice **A**) begins with an *f* sound, and *sister* (answer choice **B**) begins with an *s* sound. *Puppy* (answer choice **C**) beings with a *p* sound, just like the word *pencil*. Answer choice **D**, *cage,* begins with a hard *c* or *k* sound. Answer choice **C**, *puppy*, is the correct answer.

5

THE PLANET MARS

1   Have you ever seen the planet Mars? During some months of the year, Mars looks like a bright reddish-orange dot in the night sky. Mars is about half the size of Earth and is farther from the sun. Throughout time, people have wondered what it would be like to live on Mars. Human beings have sent spacecrafts to Mars. Some of these spacecrafts are a lot like robots. They take pictures and bring back samples of dirt from Mars. One spacecraft recorded the weather on Mars for four years.

2   We have learned a lot about Mars from these spacecrafts. Mars is different from Earth in many ways. Because Mars is so far from the sun, it is very cold there most of the time. The temperature usually does not rise above freezing. Mars has some clouds made of ice, but it has no liquid water. Mars has two moons. These moons are very small and oddly shaped. They don't look like the moon we see when we look up at the sky at night.

3   In time, we will be able to make better robots that can even teach us more about the planet Mars. One day, people will also travel to Mars. President George W. Bush set an important goal. By the year 2020, he wanted to send humans back to visit the moon. After these people visit the moon, Bush wanted them to travel to Mars. Getting to Mars won't be easy, however. It is so far away that we don't yet have a spacecraft that can take people there. But in time, we will. Maybe someday you will be one of lucky few to travel to Mars!

1 In paragraph 1, what does the word <u>recorded</u> mean?

  A Followed around
  B Watched out for
  C Kept track of
  D Looked at

This sentence asks you to choose the meaning of *recorded*. Go back and reread the sentence with this word in the selection. It says that one spacecraft recorded the weather on Mars for four years. Think about what this means. It doesn't mean that the spacecraft followed the weather around (answer choice **A**). The spacecraft did more than just watch out for the weather (answer choice **B**). It made note of what it learned about the weather so that others would know what the weather was like (answer choice **C**). While answer choice **D** might seem correct, the spacecraft did more than just look at the weather. Answer choice **C** is the best answer.

2 **The chart below shows some facts about Mars and Earth. What is another difference between Mars and Earth?**

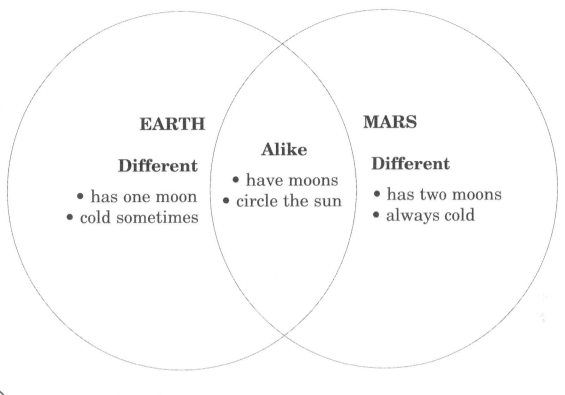

EARTH

Different

- has one moon
- cold sometimes

Alike

- have moons
- circle the sun

MARS

Different

- has two moons
- always cold

F Mars has no liquid water.
G Mars gets dark.
H Mars has stars.
J Mars has clouds.

To answer this question, you have to choose an answer choice that tells a way Mars is different from Earth. The article says that Mars does not have liquid water (answer choice **F**). This is a good answer. We know we have lots of water on Earth. It is dark on Mars (answer choice **G**), but it also get dark on Earth. We don't know from the article that Mars has stars (answer choice **H**). The article says that there are clouds on Mars (answer choice **J**). Answer choice **F** is the correct answer.

3 **How many syllables are in the word "spacecraft"?**

    A 1
    B 2
    C 3
    D 4

A *syllable* is a unit of sound that is part of a spoken word. When you speak the word *spacecraft,* how many units of sound do you hear? A word like *Mars* has only one unit of sound (answer choice **A**), or syllable. *Spacecraft* has more than one syllable. If you say the word aloud, you will hear two syllables (answer choice **B**). You can also figure out how many syllables a word has by looking that word up in a dictionary. Answer choices **C** and **D** are both incorrect. The word *spacecraft* has two syllables (answer choice **B**).

4 **This passage is mostly about —**

    F what people know about Mars
    G how President Bush set a goal
    H what Mars looks like at night
    J when people can go to Mars

This question asks you about the main idea of the passage. The passage does tell what people know about Mars (answer choice **F**), so this seems to be the correct answer. However, you should always read each answer choice first. President Bush's goal is just a detail in the article (answer choice **G**), so this is not the correct answer choice. Answer choice **H** does not tell what the whole article is about and neither does answer choice **J**, so these are not the correct answer choices.

8

5 **Which one of these questions does paragraph 3 answer?**

A Why did President Bush want to send people to the moon?

B How will people one day travel to Mars?

C How far is Mars from the moon?

D Why do people want to visit Mars?

This question asks you to ask a question about the information in one paragraph of the passage. You should choose the question that best relates to the information in the paragraph. Reread paragraph 3. It mentions that President Bush wanted to send people to the moon (answer choice **F**) before they travel to Mars, but it does not explain why, so this answer choice is incorrect. Answer choice **G** is a good answer; the paragraph discusses the fact that we will need a special spacecraft to take people to Mars. Paragraph 3 does not mention the distance between Mars and the moon (answer choice **H**), and it does not discuss why people might want to visit Mars in the first place (answer choice **J**). Answer choice **G** is the correct answer.

"MY SHADOW"

by Robert Louis Stevenson

1   I have a little shadow that goes in and out with me,

2   And what can be the use of him is more than I can see.

3   He is very, very like me from the heels up to the head;

4   And I can see him jump before me, when I jump into my bed.

5   The funniest thing abut him is the way he likes to grow—

6   Not at all like proper children, which is always very slow;

7   For he sometimes shoots up taller like an India-rubber ball,

8   And he sometimes gets so little that there's none of him at all.

9   He hasn't got a notion of how children ought to play,

10   And can only make a fool of me in every sort of way.

11   He stays so close beside me, he's a coward you can see;

12   I'd think shame to stick to nursie as that shadow sticks to me!

13   One morning, very early, before the sun was up,

14   I rose and found the shining dew on every buttercup;

15   But my lazy little shadow, like an arrant[1] sleepy head,

16   Had stayed at home behind me and was fast asleep in bed.

[1] arrant: total

---

1 What does the author's shadow do when he jumps into bed?

A gets taller
B gets little
C jumps before him
D sticks to him

You can find the answer to this question right in the poem. In the beginning of the poem, the author says, "I can see him jump before me, when I jump into my bed." Answer choice **A** says that the shadow gets taller. Sometimes the shadow does get taller, but not when the author jumps into bed. The shadow also gets smaller at times, but again, it doesn't do this when the author jumps into bed, so answer choice **B** is not the correct answer. Answer choice **C** is correct. Answer choice **D** says that the shadow sticks to the author. It does do this, but not when the author jumps into bed.

10

2 When the author gets up before the sun, the shadow —

    F shoots up taller
    G stays in bed
    H jumps up high
    J stays nearby

This question also asks about a detail in the poem. You can find this answer right in the poem. When the author gets up before the sun, his shadow stays in bed. Answer choice **G** is the correct answer. You might find some of the other answer choices in the poem, but they do not describe what the shadow does when the author gets up before the sun.

3 Which of these words from the poem rhymes with the last word in line 9?

    A head
    B ball
    C see
    D way

Find line 9 of this poem. What is the last word of line 9? Which word ends with the same sound as that word. The last word of line 9 is *play*. Answer choice **D**, *way*, ends with the same sound as *play*. Answer choice **D** is the correct answer.

4 Which list of words from the poem is in alphabetical order?

    F funniest, little, lazy, proper
    G head, heels, children, nursie
    H before, beside, behind, up
    J grow, jump, rose, stayed

This question asks you to choose the list of words that is in alphabetical order. For answer choice **F** to be correct, *lazy* would have to come before *little*; this choice is not correct. Answer choice **G** would be correct if *children* was the first word in the list, but it is not. Answer choice **H** appears to be correct, but if you look closely, you'll see that the word *behind* should come after the word *before*, so this is also an incorrect answer choice. The list of words in answer choice **J** is in alphabetical order; this is the correct answer choice.

5 **This poem is mostly about —**

    A   a boy who likes to tell funny stories
    B   a boy who teaches his shadow a lesson
    C   a boy who tells about his shadow
    D   a boy who gets up before the sun

This question asks you to tell the main idea of the poem or what the poem is mostly about. The boy does not tell funny stories (answer choice **A**). Though he talks about his shadow, he does not teach his shadow a lesson (answer choice **B**). He does tell about his shadow, so answer choice **C** is a good choice. While he does get up before the sun (answer choice **D**), this is not what the whole poem is about. Answer choice **C** is the best answer. It might also be helpful to look at the title of the poem.

6 **The author's shadow can BEST be described as —**

    F   playful
    G   angry
    H   hopeful
    J   tricky

This question asks you to choose a word that best describes the author's shadow. Reread the poem. The author does say that his shadow likes to play, so answer choice **F** might be a good answer. The author does not say that his shadow is angry (answer choice **G**), so this is not the correct answer. The author's shadow does not seem to be especially hopeful, so answer choice **H** is not the right answer. The author's shadow also is not tricky (answer choice **J**). Answer choice **F** is the best answer.

LOUIS ARMSTRONG

1   Louis Armstrong made kinds of music that people had never heard before. Louis's music was known as jazz music. The sounds of jazz made some people want to get up and dance. Jazz made other people laugh out loud or sing along. Sometimes jazz could make people think about important ideas or even cry over sad stories. Louis Armstrong was great at making all the sounds of jazz.

2   Louis was born in 1901. When he was a young man, he worked hard, and at the end of the day, he liked to rest and listen to music. He met a man named Joe "King" Oliver, who became Louis's best friend. Joe gave Louis a "cornet" (a kind of horn), which Louis could use to make his own music. Louis and Joe played together in a band and many people wanted to hear them.

3   Louis began to play music for people on boat trips and in parades. Soon, he was famous, and he traveled around the country, singing, and playing. No matter where he was, he always gave a good show. He brought people joy. All over, people enjoyed hearing his new jazz sounds. Louis even started his own bands, like the Hot Five, the Stompers, and the Allstars.

4   Jazz music remained <u>popular</u> for many years, though many people started listening to other kinds of music also. Louis worked hard to learn these new types of sounds and songs. He wanted to bring many different sounds into his own music. That way, many listeners could enjoy the songs he played. He never stopped trying to be the best musician he could be.

5   Louis had a funny nickname: "Satchmo." People gave him this name when they watched him play. When Louis blew into a horn, his face puffed up and his cheeks looked as wide as a shopping bag! People said his mouth looked like a satchel, or a bag. The nickname, "Satchel Mouth," was made shorter and soon became "Satchmo."

6   While Louis was famous, he spent much of his time helping people in need. He wanted to make sure all people were treated fairly. Many people were very sad when Louis Armstrong died in 1971, but his music and the joy he'd brought to so many never ended.

13

1 **The reader can tell that this passage is a biography because it —**

    A is about playing music
    B tells about a real person's life
    C has band names in it
    D describes a real place

What do you know about biographies and autobiographies? A biography is the story of a real person's life written by another person. An autobiography is the story of a real person's life written by that person. You can tell that this passage is a biography because it tells about the life of Louis Armstrong, who was a real person. Answer choice **B** is correct.

2 **In paragraph 4, what does the word <u>popular</u> mean?**

    F played
    G watched
    H kept
    J liked

Go back to paragraph 4 and find the sentence with the word *popular*. It says, "Jazz music remained popular for many years, though many people started listening to other kinds of music also." You can figure out the meaning of the word popular by carefully reading this sentence. It doesn't mean played (answer choice **F**). It doesn't mean watched (answer choice **G**) because you can't watch music. It could mean kept (answer choice **H**), but there's a better answer. *Popular* means liked by many (answer choice **J**).

3 **The chart below shows what happened in the story. What belongs in Box D?**

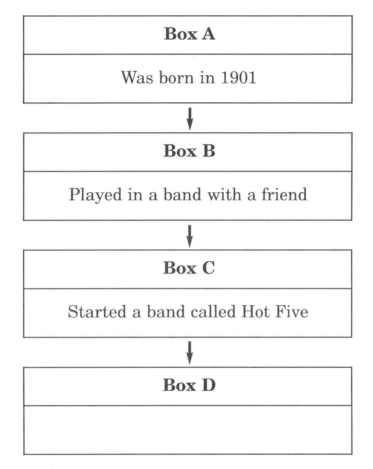

Box A

Was born in 1901

Box B

Played in a band with a friend

Box C

Started a band called Hot Five

Box D

A Brought different sounds into his music
B Started a band called the Stompers
C Learned to make his own music
D Met a man named Joe "King" Oliver

To answer this question, go back and look at the order in which things happened in the story. You need to choose the answer that is after what Armstrong did in Box C. Answer choice **A** is a good answer. Armstrong did this after he started a band called Hot Five. Answer choice **B** is not correct. The article does not say which band Armstrong started first, just that he started bands with these names. Answer choices **C** and **D** aren't correct because Armstrong did these things early in his life.

4 **What did Louis first use to make music?**

    F a cornet
    G a satchel
    H a Stomper
    J an Allstar

This question asks you to remember an idea from the passage. Each of the answer choices was in the passage, but only one of these things can make music. Read each choice carefully. Did Louis use a satchel (answer choice **G**) to make music? The passage tells us that a satchel is a bag—and bags don't make much music! Did he use a Stomper (answer choice **H**) or an Allstar (answer choice **J**) to make music? Again, no, because the passage tells us that these were names of his bands. Louis first used a cornet (answer choice **F**). The passage tells us that a cornet is a kind of horn.

5 **If Louis Armstrong were alive today, what would you most like to ask him? Use information from the article in your answer.**

     16

You have to write out your answer to this question. You might write something like this:

If Louis Armstrong were alive today, I would ask him to name his favorite song. The article says that he was a great musician and loved music. I bet he could name a song that is just beautiful. Then I would like to listen to this song.

6 **This passage is mostly about —**

    F how jazz is a popular kind of music
    G how one man became a great jazz musician
    H how many people have learned to play music
    J how horns can be hard to play

Think about what you learned from this passage. What is the most important idea that you found in the passage? The passage does say that jazz is popular (answer choice **F**), but that is just one small part of the passage. Answer choice **H** may be true, since many people do play music, but that wasn't talked about in the passage. The passage talks about Louis Armstrong playing a horn, but it doesn't say whether or not horns are hard to play (answer choice **J**). Answer choice **G** is best. The passage tells about one man, Louis Armstrong, who was a great jazz player.

ROSA'S ANT FARM

1   Rosa really wanted a new pet. She wished she could have a cat or a dog, but she lived in a large apartment building. Cats and dogs weren't allowed. Also, fur made Rosa sneeze. Her goldfish Nibbler didn't do anything interesting. Rosa's mother told her they could go buy another fish. "I don't want another fish," Rosa said. "I'm tired of watching a fish swim back and forth. I want a different kind of pet."

2   "Do you like ants?" her mother asked. "We could make an ant farm out of Nibbler's old goldfish bowl." Rosa thought that this might be fun.

3   Later that day, Rosa's mother put an empty jar inside of the goldfish bowl. She said that they were going to put the dirt around the jar. This way, Rosa would be able to see the tunnels the ants made. Rosa and her mother took a small shovel to the playground.

4   Rosa quickly spotted an ant hill. Rosa watched the ants for a while. They rushed in and out of their ant hill. "They sure seem busy," she told her mother. Then her mother dug up some dirt with ants in it. She gently placed the dirt in the bowl. The ants moved very quickly.

5   Then Rosa saw a large bug with wings near the ant hill. She was about to step on it, but her mother stopped her. "But this big bug is going to hurt the ants!" Rosa shouted.

6   "No, it won't," her mother said. "That's the queen ant. She lays the eggs." Rosa's mother put the queen on the shovel and put her in the bowl with the other ants. The little bugs began looking around at their new home.

7   "Cool," Rosa said. "These ants look like some fun pets."

8   When there was enough dirt in the bowl, Rosa's mother put the lid on top. She told Rosa to feed the ants every day. "They like bread crumbs with sugar," she said. "And you can give them a wet cotton ball for water."

9   "I'm going to keep the ant farm in my room," Rosa said, smiling.

10 "Don't move it too much. You don't want to <u>destroy</u> the ants' tunnels."

11 Rosa couldn't wait to see the ants make their tunnels in the dirt. She really liked her new pets.

1 **What important lesson does Rosa learn in this story?**

    A Ants are very busy little bugs.
    B There are many kinds of good pets.
    C Shovels are good for digging dirt.
    D Queen ants will not hurt other ants.

Rosa learns a good lesson in this story. What is it? She does learn that ants are busy bugs (answer choice **A**), since they run all over the dirt. This is not a very important lesson, though. Her mother uses a shovel to dig in the dirt (answer choice **C**), but Rosa probably already knew how to use a shovel. She did learn about queen ants (answer choice **D**), but this lesson did not change the story. The story is about how Rosa wanted a pet and found a pet she hadn't thought of before. Answer choice **B** is best. Rosa learned that there are many kinds of pets—like ants!

2 **What makes the queen ant different from the other ants?**

    F She lives in dirt.
    G She moves faster.
    H She is smaller.
    J She lays eggs.

This question asks you to tell what made one kind of ant, the queen ant, different from the other ants. If you don't remember, you can look back at the story. Look for the part of the story where Rosa finds the queen ant. Rosa's mother tells Rosa all about queen ants. All of the ants live in the dirt (answer choice **F**), so this doesn't make the queen different. Nobody says that the queen is faster (answer choice **G**). The queen is bigger than the other ants, so she can't be smaller (answer choice **H**). The thing that makes the queen different is that she lays eggs (answer choice **J**).

3   Read this sentence from the story.

> Later that day, Rosa's mother put an empty jar inside of the goldfish **b<u>owl</u>**.

Which word has the same sound as the underlined part of b<u>owl</u>?

A bounce
B hole
C both
D hope

This question asks you about word sounds, or phonetics. Say the word *bowl* in your head. What does the end of this word sound like? Which word has this same sound? *Bounce* (answer choice **A**) and *both* (answer choice **C**) begin with *bo-*, but the underlined part of bowl is at the end of the word, so this is the part we are trying to rhyme. Though the word *hole* ends in different letters than the word *bowl*, these two words still rhyme. *Hope* (answer choice **D**) does not have the same sound as the word *bowl*. Answer choice **B** is correct.

4   Before Rosa and her mother go to the playground, Rosa's mother —

F puts a jar in the bowl
G fills the bowl with dirt
H finds an ant hill
J uses a shovel

Think back to the story you've just read. Before Rosa and her mother went to the playground, Rosa's mother got some things she'd need to make an ant farm. Some of these things were a jar, a goldfish bowl, and a shovel. Once Rosa and her mother go to the playground, Rosa's mother puts dirt in the goldfish bowl (answer choice **G**). She doesn't find an ant hill (answer choice **H**) until after she gets to the playground. Then, she doesn't use the shovel (answer choice **J**) until after she finds the ant hill. The only thing Rosa's mother does *before* going to the playground is answer choice **F**, putting the jar in the goldfish bowl.

20

5   Would you like to keep ants as pets? Why or why not?

_____

_____

_____

_____

_____

_____

_____

_____

_____

_____

_____

_____

You have to write out your answer to this question. You might write something like this:

I would really like to keep ants as pets. I think it's really neat that they will build tunnels in a glass container and I would love to see the queen ant. Like Rosa, I think I would spend a lot of time watching the ants.

6   This story is mostly about —

    F a girl who sees a queen ant
    G a girl with a goldfish named Nibbler
    H a girl gets has ants for pets
    J a girl with her mother at the park

If you had to tell a friend about this story in just one sentence, what would it be? Would you say that it's about a girl seeing a queen ant (answer choice **F**)? Probably not, since that's just one small part of the story. The same goes for answer choice **G**. The author doesn't tell us much about Nibbler. Although Rosa and her mother do go to the park (answer choice **J**), that's not the biggest idea in the story. The main idea is that Rosa is a girl who gets ants for pets (answer choice **H**). Answer choice **H** tells what the whole story is about.

7   In paragraph 10, what does the word <u>destroy</u> mean?

    A break
    B make
    C help
    D find

Read these sentences carefully. Rosa's mother says them while Rosa is carrying the bowl of ants and dirt. The story tells us that the ants make tunnels. If Rosa moved the bowl too much, what might happen to these tunnels? Would moving the bowl help make the tunnels (answer choice **B**)? Probably not; the ants make the tunnels. If moving the bowl would help the tunnels (answer choice **C**), Rosa's mother probably wouldn't tell her not to move the bowl. Also, Rosa wouldn't need to move the bowl to find the tunnels, as answer choice **D** says. The best answer is answer choice **A**, *break*. If Rosa moved the bowl too much, the tunnels might break.

"THERE WAS A LITTLE GIRL"

1   There was a little girl,
2   And she had a little curl
3   Right in the middle of her forehead;
4   When she was good,
5   She was very, very good;
6   But when she was bad—she was <u>horrid</u>.

1 The little girl can BEST be described as –

A always nice
B bad at all times
C never polite
D sometimes bad

2 In line 6, what does the word <u>horrid</u> mean?

F ugly
G terrible
H sweet
J lonely

3 **Write a story about the little girl, telling about both sides of her.**

"LITTLE MISS MUFFET"

1   Little Miss Muffet
2   Sat on a tuffet,
3   Eating her curds and whey;
4   Along came a spider
5   And sat down beside her,
6   Which frightened Miss Muffet
        away.

1   This poem is mostly about –

   A   a scared girl
   B   a nice tuffet
   C   a tasty treat
   D   a fun spider

2   Why did Miss Muffet MOST likely run away?

   F   She didn't want to share.
   G   She didn't like spiders.
   H   It was beginning to rain.
   J   Her food was getting cold.

     25

3 **What would you do if a spider landed next to you? Why?**

_____

_____

_____

_____

_____

_____

_____

_____

_____

_____

_____

_____

26

FOUR POEMS

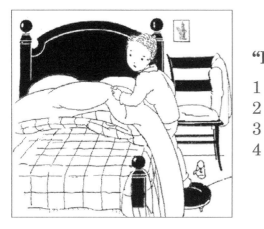

"Diddle, Diddle, Dumpling"

1   Diddle, diddle, dumpling, my son John
2   Went to bed with his <u>stockings</u> on;
3   One shoe off, the other shoe on,
4   Diddle, diddle, dumpling, my son John.

"Jack Sprat"

1   Jack Sprat could eat no fat,
2   His wife could eat no lean:
3   And so betwixt them both, you see,
4   They licked the platter clean.

"Jack and Jill"

1   Jack and Jill went up the hill
2   To fetch a pail of water;
3   Jack fell down and broke his crown,
4   And Jill came tumbling after.

"Little Jack Horner"

1   Little Jack Horner
2   Sat in a corner,
3   Eating a Christmas pie:
4   He put in his thumb
5   And pulled out a plum
6   And said, "What a good boy am I!"

27

1 What does the word <u>stockings</u> mean in line 2 of the first poem?

    A hats
    B pants
    C socks
    D shoes

2 Read this line from the second poem.

They licked the platter cl<u>ea</u>n.

Which word has the same sound as the underlined part of cl<u>ea</u>n?

    F beauty
    G dead
    H meadow
    J season

3 Why did Jack and Jill go up the hill?

    A They wanted to run down.
    B Jill was mad at Jack.
    C They wanted to get water.
    D Jack wanted a crown.

4 What will Jack Horner MOST likely do next?

    F get his mom to bake him more pie
    G eat the plum he found in his pie
    H leave the pie sitting in the corner
    J throw the pie in the garbage can

28

TWO POEMS

"There Was an Old Woman"

1. There was an old woman
2. who lived in a shoe;
3. She had so many children she
4. didn't know what to do.
5. She gave them some broth
6. without any bread,
7. And whipped them all soundly
8. and put them to bed.

"Peter, Peter, Pumpkin Eater"

1. Peter, Peter, pumpkin eater,
2. Had a wife and couldn't keep her.
3. He put her in a pumpkin shell,
4. And there he kept her very well.

1   When the old lady finished feeding her children, she –

A   cooked food for herself
B   sent the children to bed
C   looked for a new home
D   tried to fall asleep

2 **Where did Peter put his wife?**

    F in a house
    G in a shell
    H in a shoe
    J in a boat

3 **Which would you rather live in, a shoe or a pumpkin shell? Explain why.**

_____

_____

_____

_____

_____

_____

_____

_____

_____

_____

_____

_____

_____

"THIS LITTLE MOUSE"

1   This little mouse got caught in a trap,
2   And this little mouse she heard it snap,
3   This little mouse did loudly squeak out,
4   And this little mouse did run all about,
5   This little mouse said, "Do not bewail
6   And let us take hold and pull him out by the tail."

1 What is the theme of this poem?

  A Run away from danger.
  B Always listen to friends.
  C Stay away from all traps.
  D Staying calm is helpful.

2 What will the mice in the story MOST likely do next?

  F They will pull the trapped mouse out by his tail.
  G They will open up the trap the mouse was in.
  H They will get the trapped mouse to run very fast.
  J They will push the trapped mouse's head out.

3 Which list of words from the poem is in alphabetical order?

  A pull, tail, run, caught
  B heard, little, mouse, snap
  C loudly, trap, hold, by
  D about, bewail, take, squeak

31

4 **What would you do to help one of your friends who had gotten stuck? Explain your answer.**

"LITTLE BO-PEEP"

1   Little Bo-peep
2   She lost her sheep,
3   And couldn't tell where to find them.
4   "Let them alone
5   And they'll come home,
6   Wagging their tails behind them."
7   Little Bo-peep
8   Fell fast asleep
9   And dreamt she heard them bleating,
10 But when she awoke,
11 She found it a joke,
12 For still they all were <u>fleeting</u>.
13 Then up she took
14 Her little crook,
15 Determined for to find them.
16 She found them indeed,
17 But it made her heart bleed—
18 For they'd left their tails behind them.

1   In line 12, what does the word <u>fleeting</u> mean?

A   sailing
B   sleeping
C   missing
D   flying

2   After Bo Peep picked up her crook, she –

F   went back to sleep in a bed
G   went to look for the sheep
H   told someone a funny joke
J   gave up trying to find the sheep

33

3 In the poem, "Little Bo-Peep," what do you think happened to the sheep's tails?

_____

_____

_____

_____

_____

_____

_____

_____

_____

_____

_____

_____

34

WHY WOLVES AND DOGS FEAR EACH OTHER

from Lenape Stories

1   A long time ago when this world was new, the wolves and the dogs were friends. At that time, when it got to be wintertime, the wolf said, "I am cold and hungry! Who is there who would go where the humans are to get a stick with fire on one end so we could make a fire?"

2   The mongrel dog said, "Oh, my friend, I will go get some fire!"

3   The wolf said, "All right, so be it!"

4   The dog went to get the fire, saying, "We will soon have a good blazing fire! We will be warm!" So he left. He went near to where the Delaware lived. When he got near, a girl said suddenly, "Oh, there is someone who is very cute! I want to go see him. This is surely the dog." The girl began to pet the dog. She told him, "Come here, come here! You are cold! Soon I will feed you, I will give you meat and bread."

5   Oh, the dog was happy. He went into the bark house. He forgot to bring the fire. Finally the wolf gave up, saying, "That dog is a big liar! I will knock him in the head if I ever see him!" That is the reason wolves and dogs are afraid of each other to this day.

1   When the wolf said that he was cold and hungry, the dog said that he would –

   A   cook meat for the wolf
   B   find water for the wolf
   C   bring fire to the wolf
   D   bake bread for the wolf

2   **Why didn't the dog go back to the wolf?**

    F   He was so happy that he forgot about the wolf.

    G   He was too tired to leave the nice, warm house.

    H   He thought that the wolf would be upset with him.

    J   He thought that the girl would be sad if he left.

3   **Read this sentence about the passage.**

The wolf and the dog froze _____ little _____ in the snow.

    Which pair of words makes the sentence correct?

    A   their, paws

    B   there, pause

    C   their, pause

    D   there, paws

4   **Do you think some parts of this tale may be true? Why or why not? If you do think so, tell which parts you think are true.**

_____

_____

_____

_____

_____

_____

_____

_____

_____

_____

_____

_____

_____

_____

_____

_____

_____

"THE CITY MOUSE AND THE GARDEN MOUSE"

by Christina Rossetti

1 The city mouse lives in a house—
2 The garden mouse lives in a bower,
3 He's friendly with the frogs and toads,
4 And sees the pretty plants in flower.
5 The city mouse eats bread and cheese—
6 The garden mouse eats what he can;
7 We will not grudge him seeds and stalks,
8 Poor little <u>timid</u> furry man.

1 What problem does the garden mouse have?

A He does not have any friends.
B He does not have a lot of food.
C He never sees flowers or plants.
D He never gets to see the city mouse.

2 The poem is mostly about –

F a city mouse
G frogs and toads
H a garden mouse
J bread and cheese

3 In line 8, what does the word <u>timid</u> mean?

A shy
B rich
C quick
D clever

4 Which mouse does the writer seem to like best? Why?

"OLD MOTHER HUBBARD"

1   Old Mother Hubbard
2   Went to the cupboard
3   To get her poor dog a bone;
4   But when she got there,
5   The cupboard was bare,
6   And so the poor dog had none.

7   She went to the baker's
8   To buy him some bread;
9   And when she came back,
10   The poor dog was dead.

11   She went to the joiner's
12   To buy him a coffin;
13   And when she came back,
14   The doggy was laughin'.

15   She went to the butcher's
16   To buy him some tripe;
17   And when she came back,
18   He was smoking his pipe.

19   She went to the hatter's
20   To buy him a hat;
21   And when she came back,
22   He was feeding the cat.

23   She went to the barber's
24   To buy him a wig;
25   And when she came back,
26   He was dancing a jig.

27   She went to the tailor's
28   To buy him a coat;
29   And when she came back,
30   He was riding a goat.

31   She went to the cobbler's
32   To buy him some shoes;
33   And when she came back,
34   He was reading the news.

1 **At the end of the story, who was riding a goat?**

    A the butcher
    B the hatter
    C the tailor
    D the dog

2 **Read this line from the poem.**

The cupboard was <u>bare</u> . . .

    Which word rhymes with <u>bare</u>?

    F alarm
    G here
    H fair
    J laugh

3 **Do you think that the dog was funny? Why or why not?**

41

TWO POEMS WITH THE SAME TITLE

"THE WIND"
by Christina Rossetti

1   Who has seen the wind?
2   Neither you nor I
3   But when the leaves hang trembling
4   The wind is passing by.

5   Who has seen the wind?
6   Neither you nor I
7   But when the trees <u>bow</u> down their heads
8   The wind is passing by.

"THE WIND"
by Robert Louis Stevenson

1   I saw you toss the kites on high
2   And blow the birds about the sky;
3   And all around I heard you pass,
4   Like ladies' skirts across the grass—
5   O wind, a-blowing all day long,
6   O wind, that sings so loud a song!

7   I saw the different things you did,
8   But always you yourself you hid.
9   I felt you push, I heard you call,
10   I could not see yourself at all—
11   O wind, a-blowing all day long,
12   O wind, that sings so loud a song!

13   O you that are so strong and cold!
14   O blower, are you young or old?
15   Are you a beast of field and tree,
16   Or just a stronger child than me?
17   O wind, a-blowing all day long,
18   O wind, that sings so loud a song!

1   **What is the main idea the speakers in both poems say about the wind?**

   A   They have never heard wind.
   B   The wind is like a loud song.
   C   They have never seen wind.
   D   The wind makes kites move.

2   **Read this line from the poem.**

Are you a b<u>ea</u>st of field and tree . . .

   Which word has the same sound as the underlined part of b<u>ea</u>st?

   F   bird
   G   tree
   H   beg
   J   flew

3   **In line 7 of the first poem, what does the word <u>bow</u> mean?**

   A   to bend
   B   to crush
   C   a ribbon
   D   a stick

4 **Compare these two poems. How are they are same? How are they different?**

_____

_____

_____

_____

_____

_____

_____

_____

_____

_____

_____

_____

_____

_____

_____

_____

_____

_____

_____

_____

44

FOUR POEMS

by Edward Lear

1   There was an Old Man with a beard,
2   Who said, "It is just as I feared!—
3   Two Owls and a Hen, four Larks and a Wren,
4   Have all built their nests in my beard!"

1   There was an Old Person of Dean,
2   Who dined on one pea and one bean;
3   For he said, "More than that would make me too fat,"
4   That cautious Old Person of Dean.

1   There was a Young Lady whose chin
2   Resembled the point of a pin;
3   So she had it made sharp, and purchased a harp,
4   And played several tunes with her chin.

1   There is a Young Lady whose nose
2   Continually prospers and grows;
3   When it grew out of sight, she exclaimed in a fright,
4   "Oh! Farewell to the end of my nose!"

---

1   In the first poem, what was in the old man's beard?

A   dirt
B   food
C   bugs
D   birds

    45

2 Why did the Old Person of Dean eat one pea and one bean?

   F He needed to eat fewer sweet foods.
   G He didn't like to eat other foods.
   H He didn't want to eat too much.
   J He needed to eat more vegetables.

3 What lesson does the third poem teach?

   A Things aren't as bad as they seem.
   B Try to make the best of things.
   C Learn to play music.
   D Out of sight, out of mind.

4 How many syllables are in the word "exclaimed"?

   F 1
   G 2
   H 3
   J 4

"YOU ARE OLD, FATHER WILLIAM"
by Lewis Carroll

1   "You are old, father William," the young man said,
2   "And your hair has become very white;
3   And yet you incessantly stand on your head—
4   Do you think, at your age, it is right?"

5   "In my youth," father William replied to his son,
6   "I feared it might <u>injure</u> the brain;
7   But now that I'm perfectly sure I have none,
8   Why, I do it again and again."

9   "You are old," said the youth, "as I mentioned before,
10   And have grown most uncommonly fat;
11   Yet you turned a back-somersault in at the door—
12   Pray, what is the reason of that?"

13   "In my youth," said the sage, as he shook his grey locks,
14   "I kept all my limbs very supple
15   By the use of this ointment—one shilling the box—
16   Allow me to sell you a couple."

17   "You are old," said the youth, "and your jaws are too weak
18   For anything tougher than suet;
19   Yet you finished the goose, with the bones and the beak—
20   Pray, how did you manage to do it?"

47

21   "In my youth," said his father, "I took to the law,
22   And argued each case with my wife;
23   And the muscular strength, which it gave to my jaw,
24   Has lasted the rest of my life."

25   "You are old," said the youth; "one would hardly suppose
26   That your eye was as steady as ever;
27   Yet you balanced an eel on the end of your nose—
28   What made you so awfully clever?"

29   "I have answered three questions, and that is enough,"
30   Said his father; "don't give yourself airs!
31   Do you think I can listen all day to such stuff?
32   Be off, or I'll kick you down stairs!"

1   This poem is mostly about –

A a man and his wife
B a son and his father
C a nose and a brain
D an eel and a goose

2   Read this sentence from the poem.

"I feared it might <u>injure</u> the brain;

What does the word <u>injure</u> mean?

F hurt
G wake
H move
J help

    48

3 Which list of words from the story is in alphabetical order?

   A are, think, sell, William
   B use, ointment, listen, clever
   C argued, eye, said, father
   D couple, finished, suet, youth

4 How did Father William act when his son asked the last question?

"THE WALRUS AND THE CARPENTER" – Part I

by Lewis Carroll

1   The sun was shining on the sea,
2   Shining with all his might;
3   He did his very best to make
4   The billows smooth and bright—
5   And this was odd, because it was
6   The middle of the night.

7   The moon was shining sulkily,
8   Because she thought the sun
9   Had got no business to be there
10   After the day was done—
11   "It's very rude of him," she said,
12   "To come and spoil the fun!"

13   The sea was wet as wet could be,
14   The sands were dry as dry.
15   You could not see a cloud, because
16   No cloud was in the sky;
17   No birds were flying overhead—
18   There were no birds to fly.

19   The Walrus and the Carpenter
20   Were walking close at hand;
21   They wept like anything to see
22   Such quantities of sand—
23   "If this were only cleared away,"
24   They said, "it would be grand!"

25   "If seven maids with seven mops
26   Swept it for half a year,
27   Do you suppose," the Walrus said,
28   "That they could get it clear?"
29   "I doubt it," said the Carpenter,
30   And shed a bitter tear.

1   **How did the moon feel about the sun being out at night?**

   A silly
   B angry
   C happy
   D sad

2   **Read this line from the poem.**

> "If seven maids with seven <u>mops</u> . . .

   Which word rhymes with <u>mops</u>?

   F groups
   G hoops
   H soaps
   J crops

3   **What will the Walrus and the Carpenter MOST likely do next?**

   A play ball in the sand
   B run away from the rain
   C cry about the mess
   D help the maids clean

"THE WALRUS AND THE CARPENTER"
Part II
by Lewis Carroll

1   "O Oysters, come and walk with us!"
2   The Walrus did beseech.
3   "A pleasant walk, a pleasant talk,
4   Along the briny beach;
5   We cannot do with more than four,
6   To give a hand to each."

7   The eldest Oyster looked at him,
8   But never a word he said;
9   The eldest Oyster winked his eye,
10   And shook his heavy head—
11   Meaning to say he did not choose
12   To leave the Oyster bed.

13   But four young Oysters hurried up,
14   All eager for the treat;
15   Their coats were brushed, their faces washed,
16   Their shoes were clean and neat—
17   And this was odd, because, you know,
18   They hadn't any feet.

19   Four other Oysters followed them,
20   And yet another four;
21   And thick and fast they came at last,
22   And more, and more, and more—
23   All hopping through the frothy waves,
24   And scrambling to the shore.

25   The Walrus and the Carpenter
26   Walked on a mile or so,
27   And then they rested on a rock
28   Conveniently low—
29   And all the little Oysters stood
30   And waited in a row.

52

31 "The time has come," the Walrus said,
32 "To talk of many things:
33 Of shoes—and ships—and sealing wax—
34 Of cabbages—and kings—
35 And why the sea is boiling hot—
36 And whether pigs have wings."

37 "But wait a bit," the Oysters cried,
38 "Before we have our chat;
39 For some of us are out of breath,
40 And all of us are fat!"
41 "No hurry!" said the Carpenter.
42 They thanked him much for that.

43 "A loaf of bread," the Walrus said,
44 "Is what we chiefly need;
45 Pepper and vinegar besides
46 Are very good indeed—
47 Now if you're ready, Oysters dear,
48 We can begin to feed."

49 "But not on us!" the Oysters cried,
50 Turning a little blue.
51 "After such kindness, that would be
52 A dismal thing to do!"
53 "The night is fine!" the Walrus said.
54 "Do you <u>admire</u> the view?

55 "It was so kind of you to come!
56 And you are very nice!"
57 The Carpenter said nothing but,
58 "Cut us another slice.
59 I wish you were not quite so deaf—
60 I've had to ask you twice!"

61 "It seems a shame," the Walrus said.
62 "To play them such a trick,
63 After we've brought them out so far,
64 And made them trot so quick!"
65 The Carpenter said nothing but,
66 "The butter's spread too thick!"

67 "I weep for you," the Walrus said;
68 "I deeply sympathize."

69   With sobs and tears he sorted out
70   Those of the largest size,
70   Holding his pocket handkerchief
72   Before his streaming eyes.

73   "O Oysters," said the Carpenter,
74   "You've had a pleasant run!
75   Shall we be trotting home again?"
76   But answer came there none—
77   And this was scarcely odd, because
78   they'd eaten every one.

1   Why did the eldest Oyster not want to go for a walk?

A He did not trust the Walrus and the Carpenter.
B He knew he had no feet and could not walk fast.
C He was too heavy to move out of his bed.
D He did not want to leave the young Oysters behind.

2   What happened to the Oysters at the end of the poem?

F They went to sleep.
G They walked home.
H They were eaten.
J They went swimming.

3 What did the Walrus and the Carpenter do just after they walked a mile?

    A They invited the Oysters on a walk.

    B They rested on a low rock.

    C They ate a piece of bread.

    D They talked about flying pigs.

4 Read this sentence about the poem.

> **The Walrus asked the oysters, "How _____ you _____ _____ shoes?"**

    Which words make the sentence correct?

    F due, wear, you're

    G due, where, your

    H do, wear, your

    J do, where, you're

5 In line 54, what does the word <u>admire</u> mean?

    A like

    B sleep

    C laugh

    D race

55

6 **Do you think that the Walrus was really sad at the end of the passage? Explain your answer.**

_____

_____

_____

_____

_____

_____

_____

_____

_____

_____

_____

_____

WHAT'S IN A NAME?

1   Many towns in our country have oddly interesting names. Did you ever stop to think about why?

2   For example, in Alaska, there is a town called "Chicken." This town was named for a bird called the ptarmigan. Residents wanted to name their town after this bird, but they knew that the name was too complex. Instead, they named it after what the ptarmigan looked like—a chicken!

3   In Indiana, there is a town called "Santa Claus." Legend has it that residents had gathered to think of a name for their town one Christmas Eve. Suddenly, the door blew open and the sound of sleigh bells was heard. The children at the meeting yelled out, "Santa Claus! Santa Claus!" and the town got its name.

4   So, even if you've never stopped to think about where the strange name of a town came from, maybe you will now!

1 Which one of these questions does paragraph 3 answer?

    A Where in Indiana is the town of Santa Claus?
    B How did the town of Santa Claus get its name?
    C Why did people in Alaska name a town Chicken?
    D Why do many towns have such strange names?

2 This passage is mostly about –

    F a town called Chicken
    G strange birds in Alaska
    H interesting town names
    J fun places to visit

3   Read this sentence from the passage.

| Suddenly, the door <u>blew</u> open and the sound of sleigh bells was heard. |

Which one of these words sounds the same as the underlined word?

A   below
B   bowl
C   blue
D   bull

4   Think of a town with an interesting name. If you cannot think of one, make up a name. Explain how the town may have gotten its name.

_____

_____

_____

_____

_____

_____

_____

_____

_____

_____

_____

_____

58

TELLING TIME

1   Hundreds of years ago, there were no calendars to tell people what month it was. There were no clocks to tell the time of day. So how did we figure these things out?

2   Some people began to notice that the moon moved in a pattern. As a result, they invented a calendar with twelve months. Each month was made of about thirty days—the number of days in the moon's cycle!

3   People also learned something from studying the sun. They noticed that when they put a stick in the ground, it made a shadow. Throughout the day, the shadow of the sun moved around the stick. This told people what time of day it was.

4   Next, the hourglass was <u>invented</u>. The hourglass was filled with sand that slowly trickled through a hole. When you looked at it, you could tell how much time in the day had passed and how much was still left.

1   **This passage is mostly about –**

    A how readers can make a clock
    B what time it is in other places
    C why readers should buy a watch
    D how people started telling time

2   **In paragraph 4, what does the word <u>invented</u> mean?**

    F made
    G used
    H read
    J kept

59

3 **What does an hourglass use to tell time?**

  A heat
  B calendars
  C shadows
  D sand

4 **Look at this picture.**

Which word from the passage begins with the same sound?

  F moon
  G clock
  H sun
  J shadow

A DIFFERENT KIND OF JUICE

1   You've probably had apple juice, orange juice, cranberry juice, and maybe lemon juice. But what do you know about rubber juice?

2   Rubber is naturally a hard substance. When it is melted, however, can you guess what it turns into? It turns into a liquid. This liquid is called rubber juice. Rubber juice can then be poured into different molds. When these molds dry, out comes the rubber products that we use every day—raincoats, tires, boots, rubber balls, erasers, or hoses—just to name just a few.

3   So, the next time you see a fireman putting out a fire, someone bouncing a ball, or a child splashing in rain puddles, think of JUICE!

1   This passage is mostly about –

A   how rubber is made and used
B   what to wear when it is raining
C   where tires and hoses are used
D   why juice is good for drinking

2   What happens after rubber is melted?

F   It turns a different color.
G   It is poured into molds.
H   It is used to put out fires.
J   It gets very hard.

3   Read this sentence from the passage.

When it is melted, however, can you <u>gue</u>ss what it turns into?

Which word has the same vowel sound as <u>gue</u>ss?

A   blue
B   net
C   queen
D   drum

4   Think about how rubber balls bounce. What other things might be fun if they bounced like rubber balls?

62

BREAD MAKERS

1   In ancient times, seeds and nuts grew everywhere. Ancient people could gather them, store them, and eat them all year long. After a while, however, some of the people found new uses for these things. They took some of the seeds and crushed them between rocks. The substance left over was flour. This flour could then be baked under the hot sun or over a fire to make a kind of food that people could eat—bread!

2   Over time, people started trying other ingredients. They would make bread from wheat, corn, rice, and even grass. People found that bread made from these objects tasted much better than bread made from seeds and nuts. They learned to keep trying new and different ways to improve the taste and texture.

3   Soon, people started adding things like eggs, butter, sugar, milk, and yeast to the flour. Some people even added fruit and spices. Many new kinds of breads were invented by trial and error.

4   Nowadays, bread is still just as important as it was in ancient times. People all over the world eat it every day. Bread sure has come a long way!

1   **Look at this picture.**

Which word from the story begins and ends with the same sounds as the object in the picture?

A baked
B between
C bread
D butter

2 People liked wheat bread more than seed-and-nut bread because it —

  F was much healthier
  G tasted a lot better
  H cost less to make
  J was easier to find

3 The author organized the information in this passage by —

  A describing how different breads taste
  B presenting the steps needed to bake bread today
  C starting in the past and moving to today
  D explaining how to bake many kinds of bread

JELL-O

1   Jell-O®, the colorful food that most of us have eaten, is much more than just a fun dessert. This jiggly, wiggly stuff is also filled with protein, which is very good for us.

2   Jell-O is made of gelatin. Gelatin is a substance that is made from boiled-down animal skin, bones, tendons, and cartilage. That may sound gross at first but remember, these parts are filled with the protein that helps to keep us strong and healthy.

3   Once the gelatin has been made, it can be added to other ingredients to make various foods. Don't worry. Gelatin is tasteless. It is simply added to foods to thicken them up or to bind ingredients together. Foods with gelatin often have a gel-like, rubbery texture.

4   Some foods that <u>contain</u> gelatin are gummy bears, jelly, and marshmallows. Gelatin can also be found in cream cheese, soups, canned hams, and, of course, Jell-O!

1 Read this sentence from the passage.

> <u>Don't</u> worry.

Which of these is another way to write <u>don't</u>?

A did not
B does not
C do not
D dare not

2 What does the word <u>contain</u> mean in paragraph 4 of this passage?

F harden
G cook
H take
J include

3 **Which question does paragraph 3 answer?**

    A What foods have gelatin in them?

    B How is gelatin made?

    C Is gelatin healthy?

    D What does gelatin do to food?

GOING UNDERGROUND

1 Mammoth Cave in Kentucky is appropriately named. It's <u>mammoth</u> in size! The longest cave system in the world, it contains more than 335 miles of explored and mapped articleways. Scientists think that there are still hundreds of undiscovered miles in this underground cave system!

2 The Mammoth Cave system was formed by water, over thousands of years, carved through an enormous foundation of limestone. The cave was first discovered and explored by early man about 4,000 years ago. These ancient people collected crystals and salt from the limestone composition. American Indians also explored the caves and used them for centuries.

3 Modern exploration began in 1798. More than 200 species of animals have even been discovered in its depths, as well as many ancient artifacts. These findings help scientists to learn about the early Kentucky land and its people.

4 Today, Mammoth Cave is protected within the boundaries of the 50,000 acres of Mammoth Cave National Park. It is cared for by national park rangers and scientists. It is visited by thousands of tourists every year. Will you be among them?

1 How do scientists know that many people explored Mammoth Cave in the past?

  A They discovered many animals in the caves.
  B They found things that other people left behind.
  C They saw notes on the walls of the cave.
  D They were told so by the cave's park rangers.

2   Here is a list of words from the passage.

cave	limestone	scientists	exploration

If these words were in alphabetical order, which one would come THIRD?

F cave
G limestone
H scientists
J exploration

3   In paragraph 1, what does the word <u>mammoth</u> mean?

A pretty
B cold
C strong
D huge

4   What do you think that people and animals use caves for? Use information from the article to support your response.

_____

_____

_____

_____

_____

_____

_____

_____

WHAT A HISTORY!

1 Although American Indians were the first residents of New York City, it was the Dutch who put the city on the map.

2 In 1609, an English ship captain named Henry Hudson was hired by a Dutch company to explore the region. Hudson sailed into the harbor up the river that is now named for him. In doing so, he discovered Manhattan.

3 The Dutch liked the area so much that, in 1613, they took it as their own. They named it "New Amsterdam," after their beloved city in Holland.

4 In 1624, a European named Peter Minuit was put in charge of the settlement. He made a deal with the American Indians to buy the land. He paid for it with trade goods, such as furs and beads.

5 However, the Dutch did not own the land for long. In 1664, the British took it. They renamed it New York, after the Duke of York. And New York has been New York ever since!

1 What happened just after Henry Hudson discovered Manhattan?

   A The British took control of it and named it New York.
   B The Dutch took control of it and named it New Amsterdam.
   C A European man bought the land from the American Indians.
   D Henry Hudson returned to Holland to tell about his discovery.

2 Which question does paragraph 2 answer?

   F How did the Dutch pay for Manhattan?
   G Who was New York named for?
   H When did Dutch settlers move to New York?
   J How was Manhattan discovered?

3 **Read this sentence from the passage.**

They <u>re</u>named it New York, after the Duke of York.

Adding <u>re</u>- to the word named makes a word that means –

A without a name
B named for
C named again
D having two names

GLASS BLOWING

1   Today, glass bottles are a common sight. We use them for food and drink storage as well as for decoration. However, the very first glass bottles were not bought in stores. People made them through a process called "glass blowing." Yes, people actually blew air into glass!

2   The process itself was simple. A long metal tube was dipped into melted glass. Someone would then blow into the tube. The air from the person's lungs would make the glass expand, much like a balloon. After the glass took on the desired shape and size, the tube was removed. The bottle was left to cool and to harden. It could then be used as a container.

3   Of course, glass bottles are no longer made this way. Today, with advancements in technology, there are easier and faster ways to make bottles. However, there are still plenty of people who like to do it the old way. They can be found throughout the country and the world. Maybe someday you will get to see one of these glass blowers hard at work.

1   **This passage is mostly about –**

   A   why glass bottles are dangerous
   B   how readers can store food in glass
   C   how glass bottles used to be made
   D   where readers can buy glass bottles

2   **The tube was used to –**

   F   blow air into the glass
   G   make the glass melt
   H   put the glass into molds
   J   print words on the glass

3   **Read this sentence from the passage.**

Yes, people actually <u>blew</u> air into glass!

Which word rhymes with <u>blew</u>?

A know
B shoe
C draw
D row

72

TRACKS

1   Did you know that you can identify an animal simply by looking at its tracks? It's true!

2   Although all tracks may look the same at first glance, a closer look will show you that they are actually very different. While size is one factor, there are many other differences to look for.

3   Cat tracks, for example, don't show nail prints because cats keep their nails in when they walk. Dogs, on the other hand, cannot pull their nails in, so their tracks show the nail prints.

4   Deer and goat tracks look like two big toes. Horses wearing horseshoes leave the imprint of a "U," while turkey tracks take the shape of a "W." Since rabbits hop, their long hind feet land in front of their round front feet. This makes for some very odd-looking tracks!

5   Next time you come upon a <u>mysterious</u> set of tracks, take a close look. You just never know whose footsteps you might be following in!

1 Which one of these questions does paragraph 3 answer?

  A Why aren't dogs good at making tracks?
  B Why do cats pull their claws into their feet?
  C Why do dog tracks have nail prints?
  D Why are dog tracks bigger than cat tracks?

2 Read this line from the passage.

<u>Deer</u> and goat tracks look like two big toes.

Which one of these sounds the same as the underlined word?

  F dear
  G damp
  H deal
  J deep

3 In paragraph 5, what does the word <u>mysterious</u> mean?

   A peaceful

   B colorful

   C matching

   D puzzling

4 You might find animal tracks near your house.

- **What kinds of animals live near your house?**
- **What can you do to find out which animal made the tracks?**

Use information from the story to support your response.

_____

_____

_____

_____

_____

_____

_____

_____

_____

_____

_____

_____

THE CANOE

1   Long before there were motorboats and sailboats, long before there were battleships, cruise ships, rowboats and pirate boats, there was the canoe.

2   The canoe was the way that our ancestors first traveled on the water. Some of these first canoes were carved out of trees. Others were made from birch bark or animal skins stretched over a wooden frame.  Whatever they were made of, canoes were the perfect way to travel over water because they were so light. If necessary, canoes could easily be taken out of the water and carried on land without much effort.

3   In the late 1800s, canoeing became an activity that people started doing for fun. Over time, the canoe was improved. Today, many people spend their vacations peacefully paddling up and down lakes and rivers throughout the country. What a long way the canoe has come!

1   Read this sentence from the passage.

> Others were made from birch bark or animal skins stretched over a wooden frame.

Adding –en to the word wood makes a word that means —

A   filled with wood
B   too much wood
C   made of wood
D   old wood

2 A canoe might need to be picked up and carried on land to —

    F show how light it is
    G get it around a waterfall
    H test how strong it is
    J see if it was made from bark

3 This passage is mostly about —

    A a useful thing
    B a special day
    C an interesting person
    D a fun vacation

4 How many syllables are in the word canoe?

    F 1
    G 2
    H 3
    J 4

76

IN THE DESERT

1   A desert is defined as land that gets ten inches or less of rainfall per year. Because of the small amount of water, very little vegetation grows in a desert. Instead, a desert landscape is made up of sand or rocks and gravel. Some deserts also have priceless gas and oil under the ground.

2   Temperatures in hot desert regions can reach 100 degrees in the daytime. However, because the air is so dry and there are so few trees, none of that heat gets trapped. That's why temperatures can drop to forty degrees at night.

3   Deserts aren't always hot spots, though. In addition to subtropical deserts like the Sahara in Northern Africa and the Gobi in China, there are cool coastal deserts and cold winter deserts. There are even polar deserts—Antarctica is one!

4   Deserts currently make up about one-third of the earth's surface, but they're expanding all the time. In a hundred years, the earth might look a whole lot different.

1   **This passage is mostly about —**

   A   when it rains in the desert
   B   what it is like in the desert
   C   how warm it is in the desert
   D   how deserts grow over time

2   **It gets cold at night in deserts because —**

   F   there is so much ice
   G   it is so hot during the day
   H   all deserts are polar
   J   the air is so dry

3 **Read this sentence from the passage.**

> **Deserts <u>aren't</u> always hot spots, though.**

Which of these is another way to write <u>aren't</u>?

A am not
B are not
C am never
D are never

4 **What will MOST likely be different about deserts in the future?**

F They will be bigger.
G They will have more water.
H They will have more plants.
J They will be hotter.

SEASHELLS

1   Walking along a beach, you're sure to see a <u>variety</u> of beautiful seashells. However, where did they all come from?

2   Every single seashell once belonged to a mollusk. A mollusk is an animal that has no skeleton. It is soft and fragile. In order to protect itself, it grows a shell that acts as a kind of outer skeleton. Over the course of its life, a mollusk uses this shell for protection. Some mollusks even learn to use their shells as tools or as ways to help them move around.

3   When a mollusk dies, the shell is left behind. It often washes up on the seashore—where we come along and pick it up!

4   So the next time you find a seashell, you can think about the little creature that left it behind for all the world to admire.

1 Which question does paragraph 3 answer?

   A   How long does a mollusk live?
   B   Why are there seashells on the beach?
   C   How do seashells help sea animals?
   D   Why does a mollusk need a seashell?

2 Which list of words from the passage is in alphabetical order?

   F   life, mollusk, shell, skeleton
   G   move, walking, protect, use
   H   soft, fragile, beautiful, outer
   J   behind, along, up, from

3 Paragraph 2 is mostly about how mollusks —

   A   are all over the beach
   B   grow and use their shells
   C   come in many colors
   D   leave their shells behind

4 **What does the word <u>variety</u> mean in paragraph 1 of this passage?**

    F groups

    G kinds

    H sizes

    J colors

5 **Where do you think seashells come from? Use information from the article to support your response.**

BIRD CALLS

1   Do you ever think about getting a bird for a pet? If so, you might want to consider the parakeet. Parakeets make terrific pets. They don't cost a lot of money, they're easy to take care of, and they're fun to have around.

2   Most parakeets sell for just a few dollars. What a bargain! When you buy a parakeet, you will definitely get your money's worth.

3   Parakeets need only a clean cage, birdseed, fresh water, and some toys. (However, they wouldn't turn down a tasty treat as well!)

4   These little birds love to play and they love to talk. Many become completely tame and can be let outside their cages. Most parakeets love their owners and are thrilled to have attention. They also love sound. They will sing along with anything—the radio, the television, your voice—and they'll chime right in when they hear other birds.

5   If they are well cared for, parakeets can live from five to ten years. A parakeet owner will not be <u>disappointed</u>.

1 The title of this passage tells us that it is probably about —

  A where to buy the best kind of bird
  B questions to ask bird owners
  C different types of pets
  D a kind of bird that sings

2 In paragraph 5, what does the word <u>disappointed</u> mean?

  F left alone
  G asleep
  H let down
  J amazed

3 **How do parakeets learn to talk? Use information from the article to support your response.**

_____

_____

_____

_____

_____

_____

_____

_____

_____

_____

_____

_____

82

CARLOS AND JENNY – Part I

1   The rain pelted down so hard that they could hardly see. The two children ran through the heavy rain. They held their arms over their heads, but it was no use.

2   "I'm soaked!" Jenny yelled to Carlos. "My clothes are all wet!"

3   "Me, too!" Carlos yelled back. "We've got to get out of this rain and away from the lightning!"

4   He clapped his hat on his head. The two friends ran on down the muddy path. Frantically, they searched for somewhere to take shelter. All they could see was rain water pouring down a grassy hill.

5   Carlos and Jenny were at science camp. They had taken a walk to the camp headquarters, just half a mile away. Now, coming back, the short walk seemed like a 10-mile trip. They could hardly see the path before them.

6   Deep thunder rolled overhead. "Look, Carlos!" shouted Jenny. She pointed to a shadow under a huge, flat rock sticking out of the hill. She ran over to the rock. Under it was a space not big enough to stand in. Jenny kneeled down and crawled in. Carlos followed her.

7   Sitting under the rock, they caught their breath and rested. Their tiny shelter kept the rain off, but it was uncomfortable and small. Carlos turned his head and noticed a large hole behind them leading into the hill. "I bet it's nice and dry in there," he said. He crawled into the hole. Jenny shook her wet hair and crawled after him.

8   The dark shelter felt pleasantly dry and warm. "This is neat!" Carlos said.

1   What was the first thing Carlos and Jenny did in the story?

    A   looked for a large rock
    B   ran through the rain
    C   found a warm, dry shelter
    D   crawled under a rock

2 Read this sentence from the story.

| Their tiny shelter kept the rain off, but it was uncomfortable and <u>small</u>. |

Which word rhymes with <u>small</u>?

F bowl
G fail
H smooth
J hall

3 At the end of the story, Jenny can BEST be described as —

A curious
B silly
C angry
D scared

4 How did Carlos and Jenny solve their problem?

F They held their arms over their heads as they ran.
G They crawled in a hill to get out of the rain.
H They held their hats over their heads.
J They took a walk to camp headquarters.

CARLOS AND JENNY - Part II

1   Where was the cave entrance? They backed up, looking for something <u>familiar</u>. But everything was black.

2   "Oops!" Jenny bumped into Carlos, who fell down hard on the cave floor.

3   "Sorry, Carlos!" Jenny could hear Carlos brushing off his pants as he got up. "Here's my hand," she offered.

4   Carlos groped in the dark until their fingers touched. "I'm scared, Jenny. I think we're lost."

5   They stood still, listening. They could no longer hear the sound of the storm. How had they come so far inside the cave so quickly? Which way should they go to get out?

6   Out of the silence, they heard the trickling sound of water. It sounded like a small stream, along with dripping sounds. Was it raining that hard outside?

7   Flap! Flap! Flap! "What was that?" cried Carlos.

8   "Something flew over my head!" Jenny screamed. "Something's flying around in here." She waved her arms over her head.

9   Squeak! Squeak! Squeak! The two children looked up toward the sound. They couldn't see anything, but a tiny voice squeaked at them. *Calm down! I'm just over your head. Be careful!*

10   "Huh?" Carlos reached up. His fingers briefly touched a small, warm animal with short, silky fur.

11   *Don't touch me!* said the squeaky voice.

12   "I don't want to touch you!" Carlos said. "What are you?"

13   *I'm a bat, of course. Who else would be flying around in a cave? Batman?*

14   Carlos and Jenny both laughed. They explained to the bat that they were lost and had to get back to science camp. Could the bat help?

15   There was a long silence. The two friends realized that this bat could be their only hope of getting out of the cave. Would he help them?

16   Finally, the squeaky voice replied, *I guess I'll help you. I like talking to people. I can take you to another cave entrance that will be a shortcut to your camp. That way you can stay out of the rain. I can show you the rest of the cave, too.*

17   Carlos wanted to go right back to camp, but he loved adventures. Besides, it was probably still pouring rain out there. "Gee, Bat, that would be great. I'd love to see the cave, too."

1 **What does the word <u>familiar</u> mean in paragraph 1 of this story?**

   A scary

   B common

   C hard

   D beautiful

2 **When the bat first flew over Jenny's head, Jenny —**

   F touched the bat

   G screamed

   H swung at the bat

   J laughed

3 **What will Carlos and Jenny MOST likely do next?**

   A go back outside

   B follow the bat

   C talk to another bat

   D scare the bat

4 **Read this sentence about the passage.**

> **If Carlos and Jenny had not crawled in the _____, they would not have _____ the inside of the cave.**

   Which pair of words makes the sentence correct?

   F whole, scene

   G hole, scene

   H whole, seen

   J hole, seen

CARLOS AND JENNY – Part III

1   "Stop! Jenny, look back there!" Carlos pointed to the wall. The flashlight lit up a series of pale figures. The two friends stared. A row of eight dark handprints appeared on the wall. They looked like fingerprint figures made of dark clay or mud. On the left were the smallest prints—those of a child. On the right, adults had left larger marks.

2   "Whose hands were those?" Jenny wondered.

3   "Look over there." Carlos pointed. "Animal paintings. These things are old."

4   Jenny studied the paintings, beautifully outlined in black. She agreed. It looked as if the artists had drawn the pictures with the ashes of a campfire, long, long ago. She could almost hear their voices in the cave.

5   A buffalo, in soft brown and orange colors, commanded the wall. Below the buffalo, a deer with antlers leaped high. It was badly wounded, with three arrows in its chest.

6   "American Indians," murmured Carlos. "Maybe these are the same tribes that we studied about in school, like the really old people they found signs of in Mammoth Cave."

7   They looked again in silence. They forgot all about the bat, who suddenly flapped over their heads.

8   *Thank you! Thank you!* the bat squeaked. *I've lived in this cave all my life and have never seen these pictures. If you hadn't come with the flashlight, I would never have actually seen them. Thank you!*

9   The two children looked up at Bat, pleased and surprised. They felt happy that they could give something back to this little animal who was saving their lives. Bat hung on a rock overhead, looking at the pictures.

10   Together they stared at the ancient pictures. Why did these people come to this cave? Perhaps it was warm here in the winter and cool in the summer. Did they live here all the time or just in bad weather? Were the handprints a family? Or members of a tribe? What happened to them?

11   Jenny spread her fingers near the smallest print, afraid to touch it. She held her hands in the air, matching thumb to thumb, pinky to pinky. Her hands were just a little bigger than the prints. Was this a boy, like Carlos? Or a girl, like her? If so, how old was she? What was her name?

12   Carlos looked at the animals. He saw the arrows in the deer's chest and even a line showing blood. These were hunting people.

13   "Bat, how old are these American Indian things?" Jenny asked.

14 *Oh, I don't know. I bet thousands of years,* Bat squeaked.

15 "But why haven't cave explorers found these things, Bat?"

16 *They might have, and they were careful not to touch or destroy them. But maybe they couldn't get in here because they were grown-ups. You kids got through that skinny tunnel more easily. It's pretty small for grown-ups. I bet those people from long ago were really small, too.*

1 Read this sentence from the story.

Jenny studied the paintings, beautifully outlined in black.

Which word in the sentence tells what someone did?

A Jenny
B studied
C paintings
D beautifully

2 What question does paragraph 4 answer?

F What were the cave paintings most likely drawn with?
G Why are the cave walls covered in paintings?
H Why would a child put a handprint on a cave wall?
J What should Carlos and Jenny tell people about the cave?

3 Read this sentence from the story.

The two children looked up at Bat, p<u>lease</u>d and surprised.

Which word has the same sound as the underlined part of p<u>lease</u>d?

A half
B trot
C cheese
D fault

4 **Which BEST describes how Carlos and Jenny felt about finding the paintings?**

F saddened
G tired
H surprised
J afraid

5 **Bat thought that no one had seen the paintings before because —**

A the cave was too small for grown-ups
B no one had been in the cave before
C he had frightened the grown-ups away
D there wasn't any light inside the cave

6 **If people lived in that part of the cave, what other things might Carlos and Jenny find? Use complete sentences to explain your answer.**

"TREES"

by Joyce Kilmer

1   I think that I shall never see

2   A poem lovely as a tree.

3   A tree whose hungry mouth is prest

4   Against the earth's sweet flowing breast;

5   A tree that looks at God all day,

6   And lifts her leafy arms to pray;

7   A tree that may in Summer wear

8   A nest of robins in her hair;

9   Upon whose bosom snow has lain;

10   Who intimately lives with rain.

11   Poems are made by fools like me,

12   But only God can make a tree.

1   **The author compares a tree to –**

A the sky

B a poem

C the spring

D a rainy day

2   **What is the theme of this poem?**

F The most beautiful things are found in nature.

G Trees need a lot of rain and sunshine to live.

H Trees are much nicer to look at than poems.

J Nothing is more beautiful than a snowy tree.

Here is part of a table of contents. Use it to answer the next question.

3   **Which poem begins on page 16?**

A   "Trees"
B   "My Shadow"
C   "The Lamplighter"
D   "Paul Revere's Ride"

4   **Do you think this is a good poem? Why or why not?**

"ALARM CLOCKS"

by Joyce Kilmer

1   When Dawn strides out to wake a dewy farm
2   Across green fields and yellow hills of hay
3   The little twittering birds laugh in his way
4   And poise triumphant on his shining arm.
5   He bears a sword of flame but not to harm
6   The wakened life that feels his quickening sway
7   And barnyard voices shrilling "It is day!"
8   Take by his grace a new and alien charm.
9   But in the city, like a wounded thing
10 That limps to cover from the angry chase,
11 He <u>steals</u> down streets where sickly arc-lights sing,
12 And wanly mock his young and shameful face;
13 And tiny gongs with cruel fervor ring
14 In many a high and dreary sleeping place.

1   **In line 11, what does the word <u>steals</u> mean?**

   A takes away
   B goes secretly
   C makes use of
   D wins unfairly

2   **Which of these words from the poem rhymes with the last word in line 9?**

   F chase
   G sing
   H voices
   J streets

3 **In this poem, the poet talks about dawn in both the city and the country.**

- **Explain how the poet feels about dawn in each place.**
- **Decide which one is better and explain why.**

_____

_____

_____

_____

_____

_____

_____

_____

_____

_____

_____

_____

_____

_____

_____

_____

_____

_____

93

from "THE VILLAGE BLACKSMITH"

by Henry Wadsworth Longfellow (1807–1882)

1   Under a spreading chestnut tree
2   The village smithy stands;
3   The smith, a mighty man is he,
4   With large and sinewy hands;
5   And the muscles of his brawny arms
6   Are strong as iron bands.
7   His hair is crisp, and black, and long,
8   His face is like the tan;
9   His brow is wet with honest sweat,
10   He earns whate'er he can,
11   And looks the whole world in the face,
12   For he owes not any man.
13   Week in, week out, from morn till night,
14   You can hear his bellows blow;
15   You can hear him swing his heavy sledge
16   With measured beat and slow,
17   Like a sexton ringing the village bell,
18   When the evening sun is low.
19   And children coming home from school
20   Look in at the open door;
21   They love to see the flaming forge,
22   And hear the bellows roar,
23   And watch the burning sparks that fly
24   Like chaff from a threshing-floor.
25   He goes on Sunday to the church,
26   And sits among his boys;
27   He hears the parson pray and preach,
28   He hears his daughter's voice,
29   Singing in the village choir,
30   And it makes his heart rejoice.
31   It sounds to him like her mother's voice,
32   Singing in Paradise!
33   He needs must think of her once more,
34   How in the grave she lies;
35   And with his hard, rough hand he wipes
36   A tear out of his eyes.

1 Read this line from the poem.

> He hears his daughter's v<u>oi</u>ce . . .

Which word has the same sound as the underlined part of v<u>oi</u>ce?

A boys
B juice
C cough
D seize

2 The blacksmith can BEST be described as –

F smart
G funny
H brave
J strong

3 This poem is mostly about –

A the lives of the children
B the life of the blacksmith's wife
C the life of a sexton
D the life of the blacksmith

4 The children can see the blacksmith work because they –

F watch from the school windows
G look into his blacksmith shop
H see him with his daughter
J imagine what it is like

5   In the poem, the poet writes about children watching the blacksmith work.

- Write about someone who works with his or her hands that you either like to watch or think you might like to watch.
- Explain who this person is and why you like to watch him or her at work.

_____

_____

_____

_____

_____

_____

_____

_____

_____

_____

_____

_____

_____

_____

EDWARD THE BRAVE

1   Edward Kennedy, Jr. is someone we can all admire. When he was just a child, he was told that he had cancer in one of his legs. The doctor said that, in order to save his life, Edward's leg would have to be taken off. Edward was scared, but he did what he had to do.

2   Edward survived and grew strong and healthy. A new leg was made for him. Not only did Edward learn how to walk with his new leg, he learned how to do many other things as well. Eventually, he learned to swim, climb mountains, ride a bike, and ski.

3   Edward never forgot his experience. When he grew up, he decided that he wanted to help other children who had cancer. He wanted them to know that they could overcome the challenge of being sick and scared. Edward started a group called the "I can do it" group. Now, thanks to Edward, the sky is the limit for these special children.

1 The reader can tell that this passage is a biography because it –

  A tells about a real person's life
  B is about learning to climb mountains
  C describes a special group for kids
  D was written by Edward Kennedy, Jr.

2 Which question does paragraph 3 answer?

  F How did Edward learn to walk?
  G Why did Edward start a group for kids?
  H What happened to Edward's leg?
  J What kinds of things did Edward like to do?

3 Edward's leg was removed because –

  A he did not walk
  B he had cancer
  C it was too short
  D it was broken

4 Many people today get new legs, hips, or knees. Explain how this is helpful to people. Decide what you think could happen in the future to solve this problem and why.

IT'S ALL IN THE TRUNK

1   An elephant's trunk is very useful. In fact, an elephant depends upon its trunk for more than you might think.

2   First, an elephant breathes and smells through its trunk. It even uses its trunk as a snorkel when it's swimming underwater!

3   This mighty beast also speaks through the trunk. In fact, it can change the sound of its voice by making the nostrils bigger and smaller. This lets elephants communicate with each other in different ways.

4   It also uses its massive trunk to suck up water, which it can then spray over itself for a shower—or into its mouth for a drink. It can also spray dust on itself to keep flies from biting.

5   Finally, the elephant can use its trunk to move things. The trunk is strong and flexible. It can lift heavy logs to move them out of the way or pull branches out of tall trees for a leafy meal. Two finger-like objects on the tip allow this giant to even pick up the smallest of items, such as peanuts—a favorite treat. Now that's an impressive trunk!

1   Look at this dictionary entry for the word trunk.

trunk (truhngk) *n.* **1.** the main stem of a tree **2.** part of the human body including the chest, stomach, and back **3.** the rear part of a car used to store or carry things **4.** a large, flexible snout or nose **5.** a large piece of luggage

Which meaning of the word trunk is used in this passage?

A   the main stem of a tree
B   the rear part of a car used to store or carry things
C   a large, flexible snout or nose
D   a large piece of luggage

99

2 How many syllables are in the word "elephant"?

   F 1

   G 2

   H 3

   J 4

3 Which question does paragraph 3 answer?

   A How do elephants communicate?

   B How do elephants move things?

   C How do elephants stay clean?

   D How do elephants drink water?

4 Do you think it might be fun to have a trunk? What would you use a trunk to do?

_____

_____

_____

_____

_____

_____

_____

_____

_____

_____

WASP

1   During World War II, women were given a chance to do something they had never before been allowed to do—fly for the Air Force!

2   The idea came from a woman named Jacqueline Cochran. Cochran had heard that there were not enough male combat pilots in the Army Air Force. She wrote a letter to the president's wife in which she presented the idea that women be trained to fly.

3   The army liked this idea. As a result, 25,000 women applied to become pilots. Of this huge number, 1,830 were accepted into training. Of these, 1,074 graduated from a <u>difficult</u> training course. This group became the Women Air Force Service Pilots, better known as WASP.

4   For the last two years of World War II, WASP flew service planes for the Army Air Force. They transported soldiers, participated in tests and simulations, flew demonstration flights, and became flight instructors. Their work allowed the army to send more of their male pilots into combat. This helped the United States to win.

5   When the war ended, all the women had to return to their regular lives. Even though their work had lasted for only a short time, these women will be remembered for their brave service to their country in a time of war.

1 How did Jacqueline Cochran solve the Army Air Force's problem of not having enough men to fly planes during World War II?

A She gave them money to hire more pilots.
B She suggested that women be trained to fly planes.
C She asked the president to give them more planes.
D She set up a program to teach people how to fly planes.

2 The women in the Army Air Force during World War II can BEST be described as –

F scared
G helpful
H foolish
J angry

3 In paragraph 3, what does the word <u>difficult</u> mean?

   A cold
   B dark
   C hard
   D slow

4 Do you think that you would like to learn to fly a plane? Why or why not?

_____

_____

_____

_____

_____

_____

_____

_____

_____

_____

_____

_____

YEE-HA?

1   Despite how much fun it may look on television and in the movies, being a cowboy or a cowgirl is hard work!

2   You have to get up at the crack of dawn to round up the cows. You have to ride your horse all day long, making sure to keep those cows in line. This isn't easy. The sun is hot, the air is dry, and there is not a lot of shade. You get tired very fast, but you can't go to sleep until late at night.

3   Driving cattle is not your only job. You also have to dig wells and <u>mend</u> fences. You have to know where you are at all times and you have to watch the sky for bad weather. You have to be sure that you and the animals stay healthy and strong. You do all this for very little money.

4   The payoff, though, is big in other ways. It's in the relationship you have with your horse, your best friend and companion. It's the chance to work under the big sky and to sleep under the stars in the freshest air you've ever breathed. It's the chance to be one with the land. Would you do it?

1 This passage is mostly about –

   A how cowgirls get their jobs
   B the lives of cowboys and cowgirls
   C which jobs are most dangerous
   D the best way to care for cows

2 Most people think that being a cowboy or cowgirl is fun because –

   F it looks easy in the movies
   G the horse does all the work
   H it does not take much time
   J the horses like to play a lot

3 Cowboys and cowgirls can BEST be described as –

A happy
B strong
C fun
D angry

4 In paragraph 3, what does the word <u>mend</u> mean?

F climb
G jump
H start
J fix

LADY JUDGE

1   Sandra Day O'Connor was the very first female justice to serve on the Supreme Court of the United States. Those who knew her as a youngster were not surprised one bit.

2   Sandra had been a smart child. She skipped grades and finished high school when she was only sixteen years old. She graduated from college and law school with high honors. Despite her excellent grades, however, it was hard for her to get a job. In those days, not too many companies hired female lawyers.

3   Sandra worked hard anyway. She worked her way up the ladder and people came to notice and respect her. Eventually, even the president of the United States noticed. He appointed her to the highest court in the land—the Supreme Court. She served on this court from 1981 until 2006 when she retired. Today, she is enjoying a well-deserved retirement, living happily with her husband at their home in Arizona.

1 This passage is mostly about –

   A working with others
   B an interesting person
   C learning to be a judge
   D finding a great job

2 What is the theme of this passage?

   F Kids can finish school early.
   G Reading can be lots of fun.
   H Never give up on a dream.
   J Help others when you can.

3 **When Sandra was sixteen, she –**

   A became a lawyer
   B met with the president
   C finished high school
   D became a judge

4 **What will Sandra Day O'Connor MOST likely be remembered for doing?**

   F having three sons
   G going to college
   H becoming a lawyer
   J becoming a judge

from "THE PRINCESS AND THE GOBLIN"
Part I
by George MacDonald

CHAPTER 3: The Princess and—We Shall See Who

1   "Do you know my name, child?"

2   "No, I don't know it," answered the princess.

3   "My name is Irene."

4   "That's my name!" cried the princess.

5   "I know that. I let you have mine. I haven't got your name. You've got mine."

6   "How can that be?" asked the princess, bewildered. "I've always had my name."

7   "Your papa, the king, asked me if I had any objection to your having it; and, of course, I hadn't. I let you have it with pleasure."

8   "It was very kind of you to give me your name—and such a pretty one," said the princess.

9   "Oh, not so very kind!" said the old lady. "A name is one of those things one can give away and keep all the same. I have a good many such things. Wouldn't you like to know who I am, child?"

10   "Yes, that I should—very much."

11   "I'm your great-great-grandmother," said the lady.

12   "What's that?" asked the princess.

13   "I'm your father's mother's father's mother."

14   "Oh, dear! I can't understand that," said the princess.

15   "I dare say not. I didn't expect you would. But that's no reason why I shouldn't say it."

16   "Oh, no!" answered the princess.

17   "I will explain it all to you when you are older," the lady went on. "But you will be able to understand this much now: I came here to take care of you."

18   "Is it long since you came? Was it yesterday? Or was it today, because it was so wet that I couldn't get out?"

19   "I've been here ever since you came yourself."

107

20   "What a long time!" said the princess. "I don't remember it at all."

21   "No. I suppose not."

22   "But I never saw you before."

23   "No. But you shall see me again."

24   "Do you live in this room always?"

25   "I don't sleep in it. I sleep on the opposite side of the landing. I sit here most of the day."

26   "I shouldn't like it. My nursery is much prettier. You must be a queen too, if you are my great big grand-mother."

27   "Yes, I am a queen."

28   "Where is your crown, then?"

29   "In my bedroom."

30   "I should like to see it."

31   "You shall some day—not today."

32   "I wonder why nursie never told me."

33   "Nursie doesn't know. She never saw me."

34   "But somebody knows that you are in the house?"

35   "No; nobody."

36   "How do you get your dinner, then?"

37   "I keep poultry—of a sort."

38   "Where do you keep them?"

39   "I will show you."

40   "And who makes the chicken broth for you?"

41   "I never kill any of MY chickens."

42   "Then I can't understand."

43   "What did you have for breakfast this morning?" asked the lady.

44   "Oh! I had bread and milk, and an egg—I dare say you eat their eggs."

45   "Yes, that's it. I eat their eggs."

46   "Is that what makes your hair so white?"

47   "No, my dear. It's old age. I am very old."

108

48 "I thought so. Are you fifty?"

49 "Yes—more than that."

50 "Are you a hundred?"

51 "Yes—more than that. I am too old for you to guess. Come and see my chickens."

1 The old lady can BEST be described as —

A mean
B strange
C small
D happy

2 What was the first thing the old lady and the princess talked about?

F the lady's home
G their names
H breakfast food
J a nursery

3 What question does paragraph 17 answer?

A What did the princess eat for breakfast?
B When does the princess visit her nursery?
C How is the old lady meeting the princess?
D Why did the old lady visit the princess?

4 Read this sentence from the story.

"Is that what makes your hair so <u>white</u>?"

Which word rhymes with <u>white</u>?

F late
G eight
H mitt
J fight

5 How many syllables are in the word "prettier"?

A 1
B 2
C 3
D 4

6 Read this sentence about the passage.

An old lady _____ her _____ granddaughter.

Which pair of words makes the sentence correct?

F seas, great-great
G seas, grate-grate
H sees, great-great
J sees, grate-grate

110

7 **Do you think that the old lady is lying to the princess? Why or why not? Use details from the passage to explain your answer.**

_____

_____

_____

_____

_____

_____

_____

_____

_____

_____

_____

_____

_____

_____

_____

_____

from "THE RAILWAY CHILDREN" – Part I
by Edith Nesbit

1   "Look what a great mound it's made!" said Bobbie.

2   "Yes," said Peter, slowly. He was still leaning on the fence. "Yes," he said again, still more slowly.

3   Then he stood upright.

4   "The 11:29 down hasn't gone by yet. We must let them know at the station, or there'll be a most frightful accident."

5   "Let's run," said Bobbie, and began.

6   But Peter cried, "Come back!" and looked at Mother's watch. He was very prompt and businesslike, and his face looked whiter than they had ever seen it.

7   "No time," he said; "it's two miles away, and it's past eleven."

8   "Couldn't we," suggested Phyllis, breathlessly, "couldn't we climb up a telegraph post and do something to the wires?"

9   "We don't know how," said Peter.

10 "They do it in war," said Phyllis; "I know I've heard of it."

11 "They only cut them, silly," said Peter, "and that doesn't do any good. And we couldn't cut them even if we got up, and we couldn't get up. If we had anything red, we could get down on the line and wave it."

12 "But the train wouldn't see us till it got round the corner, and then it could see the mound just as well as us," said Phyllis; "better, because it's much bigger than us."

13 "If we only had something red," Peter repeated, "we could go round the corner and wave to the train."

14 "We might wave, anyway."

15 "They'd only think it was just us, as usual. We've waved so often before. Anyway, let's get down."

16 They got down the steep stairs. Bobbie was pale and shivering. Peter's face looked thinner than usual. Phyllis was red-faced and damp with anxiety.

17 "Oh, how hot I am!" she said; "and I thought it was going to be cold; I wish we hadn't put on our—" she stopped short, and then ended in quite a different tone—"our flannel petticoats."

18 Bobbie turned at the bottom of the stairs.

19 "Oh, yes," she cried; "they're red! Let's take them off."

1 **What will the children MOST likely do next?**

    A use the petticoats to get the driver to stop the train
    B climb up the pole and cut the wires
    C run quickly to the train station
    D wave to the driver of the train as he passes by

2 **What did Phyllis find?**

    F something red
    G warmer coats
    H how to get home
    J what time it is

3 **Read this line from the passage.**

> " . . . I wish we <u>hadn't</u> put on our—" she stopped short, and then ended in quite a different tone—"our flannel petticoats."

    Which of these is another way to write <u>hadn't</u>?

    A had never
    B had not
    C hardly ever
    D have not

4 **Why wouldn't waving at the train force it to stop?**

    F Too much smoke would hide the children from sight.
    G Many people waved to the train as it passed.
    H The conductor would not see because he was blind.
    J The train was going much too fast to see them.

from "POLLYANNA"

by Eleanor H. Porter

1   "I'm a stranger to you, of course," she began at once. "But I'm not a stranger to your little niece, Pollyanna. I've been at the hotel all summer, and every day I've had to take long walks for my health. It was on these walks that I've met your niece—she's such a dear little girl! I wish I could make you understand what she's been to me. I was very sad when I came up here; and her bright face and cheery ways reminded me of—my own little girl that I lost years ago. I was so shocked to hear of the accident; and then when I learned that the poor child would never walk again, and that she was so unhappy because she couldn't be glad any longer—the dear child!—I just had to come to you."

2   "You are very kind," murmured Miss Polly.

3   "But it is you who are to be kind," demurred the other. "I—I want you to give her a message from me. Will you?"

4   "Certainly."

5   "Will you just tell her, then, that Mrs. Tarbell is glad now. Yes, I know it sounds odd, and you don't understand. But—if you'll pardon me I'd rather not explain." Sad lines came to the lady's mouth, and the smile left her eyes. "Your niece will know just what I mean; and I felt that I must tell—her. Thank you; and pardon me, please, for any seeming rudeness in my call," she begged, as she took her leave.

6   Thoroughly mystified now, Miss Polly hurried up-stairs to Pollyanna's room.

7   "Pollyanna, do you know a Mrs. Tarbell?"

8   "Oh, yes. I love Mrs. Tarbell. She's sick, and awfully sad; and she's at the hotel, and takes long walks. We go together. I mean—we used to." Pollyanna's voice broke, and two big tears rolled down her cheeks.

9   Miss Polly cleared her throat hurriedly.

10 "We'll, she's just been here, dear. She left a message for you—but she wouldn't tell me what it meant. She said to tell you that Mrs. Tarbell is glad now." Pollyanna clapped her hands softly.

11 "Did she say that—really? Oh, I'm so glad!"

12 "But, Pollyanna, what did she mean?"

13 "Why, it's the game, and—" Pollyanna stopped short, her fingers to her lips.

14 "What game?"

15 "N-nothing much, Aunt Polly; that is—I can't tell it unless I tell other things that—that I'm not to speak of."

114

16   It was on Miss Polly's tongue to question her niece further; but the obvious distress on the little girl's face stayed the words before they were uttered.

1   What was wrong with Pollyanna?

   A   She couldn't walk.
   B   She was very sad.
   C   She was very sick.
   D   She couldn't talk.

2   Which one of these questions does paragraph 8 answer?

   F   What month is it in the story?
   G   How old is Pollyanna?
   H   Who is Mrs. Tarbell?
   J   What time of day is it?

3   Read this sentence from the story.

> It was on Miss Polly's tongue to question her niece further; but the obvious distress on the little girl's face stayed the words before they were uttered.

   Which word has the same sound as the underlined part of niece?

   A   birth
   B   eighty
   C   inquire
   D   freeze

115

4 **At the end of the story, Miss Polly felt —**

   F curious

   G happy

   H upset

   J bored

from "AT THE BACK OF THE NORTH WIND"

by George MacDonald

1 The next instant a young girl glided across the bed, and stood upon the floor.

2 "Oh dear!" said Diamond, quite dismayed; "I didn't know—who are you, please?"

3 "I'm North Wind."

4 "Are you really?"

5 "Yes. Make haste."

6 "But you're no bigger than me."

7 "Do you think I care about how big or how little I am? Didn't you see me this evening? I was less then."

8 "No. Where was you?"

9 "Behind the leaves of the primrose. Didn't you see them blowing?"

10 "Yes."

11 "Make haste, then, if you want to go with me."

12 "But you are not big enough to take care of me. I think you are only Miss North Wind."

13 "I am big enough to show you the way, anyhow. But if you won't come, why, you must stay."

14 "I must dress myself. I didn't mind with a grown lady, but I couldn't go with a little girl in my night-gown."

15 "Very well. I'm not in such a hurry as I was the other night. Dress as fast as you can, and I'll go and shake the primrose leaves till you come."

16 "Don't hurt it," said Diamond.

17 North Wind broke out in a little laugh like the breaking of silver bubbles, and was gone in a moment. Diamond saw—for it was a starlit night, and the mass of hay was at a low ebb now—the gleam of something vanishing down the stair and, springing out of bed, dressed himself as fast as ever he could.

18 Then he crept out into the yard, through the door in the wall, and away to the primrose. Behind it stood North Wind, leaning over it, and looking at the flower as if she had been its mother.

19 "Come along," she said, jumping up and holding out her hand.

20 Diamond took her hand. It was cold, but so pleasant and full of life, it was better than warm. She led him across the garden. With one bound she was on the top of the wall. Diamond was left at the foot.

21   "Stop, stop!" he cried. "Please, I can't jump like that."

22   "You don't try," said North Wind, who from the top looked down a foot taller than before.

23   "Give me your hand again, and I will try," said Diamond.

24   She reached down. Diamond laid hold of her hand, gave a great spring, and stood beside her.

25   "This is nice!" he said.

1   **Read this sentence from the story.**

> "You don't <u>try</u>," said North Wind, who from the top looked down a foot taller than before.

Which word rhymes with <u>try</u>?

A hurry
B lonely
C plenty
D fly

2   **When Diamond saw the North Wind, he felt —**

F scared
G surprised
H unhappy
J tired

3   **In paragraph 17, what does the word <u>vanishing</u> mean?**

A looking
B walking
C disappearing
D moving

THE CAT AND THE MOUSE

1   *The cat and the mouse*

Played in the malt-house:

2   The cat bit the mouse's tail off. "Pray, puss, give me my tail."

3   "No," says the cat, "I'll not give you your tail. Not until you go to the cow and fetch me some milk."

4   *First she leapt, and then she ran,*

Till she came to the cow, and thus began—

5   "Pray, cow, give me milk, that I may give cat milk, that cat may give me my own tail again."

6   "No," said the cow, "I will give you no milk. Not until you go to the farmer and get me some hay."

7   *First she leapt, and then she ran,*

Till she came to the farmer, and thus began—

8   "Pray, farmer, give me hay that I may give cow hay, that cow may give me milk, that I may give cat milk, that cat may give me my own tail again."

9   "No," says the farmer, "I'll give you no hay. Not until you go to the butcher and fetch me some meat."

10   *First she leapt, and then she ran,*

Till she came to the butcher, and thus began—

11   "Pray, butcher, give me meat, that I may give farmer meat, that farmer may give me hay, that I may give cow hay, that cow may give me milk, that I may give cat milk, that cat may give me my own tail again."

12   "No," says the butcher, "I'll give you no meat. Not until you go to the baker and fetch me some bread."

13   *First she leapt, and then she ran,*

Till she came to the baker, and thus began—

14   "Pray, baker, give me bread, that I may give butcher bread, that butcher may give me meat, that I may give farmer meat, that farmer may give me hay, that I may give cow hay, that cow may give me milk, that I may give cat milk, that cat may give me my own tail again."

15   "Yes," says the baker, "I'll give you some bread, but if you eat my meal, I'll cut off your head."

119

16   Then the baker gave mouse bread. The mouse gave butcher bread. The
      butcher gave mouse meat. The mouse gave farmer meat. The farmer gave
      mouse hay. The mouse gave cow hay. The cow gave mouse milk. The mouse
      gave cat milk. The cat gave mouse her own tail again!

1   **When the cat bit off the mouse's tail, the cat —**

     A ate the mouse's tail
     B asked for some milk
     C laughed at the mouse
     D ran away and hid

2   **This story is mainly about —**

     F an unhappy cat that bit off a tail
     G a busy farmer who wanted some hay
     H a mouse that wanted its tail back
     J a cow that wanted some fresh bread

3   **What did the farmer want the mouse to get?**

     A milk
     B meat
     C bread
     D hay

120

4 **How did the author show that the mouse's tail is important to her? Use information from the passage to support your answer.**

_____

_____

_____

_____

_____

_____

_____

_____

_____

_____

_____

_____

_____

_____

_____

_____

_____

HOW COYOTE GOT HIS SPECIAL POWER

1   In the beginning of the world, Spirit Chief called a meeting of all the animal people.

2   "Some of you do not have names yet," he said when they had gathered together. "And some of you do not like the names you have now.

3   "Tomorrow, before the sun rises I will give a name to everyone. And I will give each an arrow also.

4   "Come to my lodge as soon as the darkness is gone. The one who gets there first may choose any name he wants. I will give him the longest arrow. The longest arrow will mean that he will have the most power."

5   As the people left the meeting, Coyote said to his friend Fox, "I'm going to be there first. I don't like my name. I want to be called Grizzly Bear or Eagle."

6   Fox laughed. "No one wants your name. You may have to keep it."

7   "I'll be there first," repeated Coyote. "I won't go to sleep tonight."

8   That night he sat by his fire. He stayed awake for a long time. Owl hooted at him. Frog croaked in the marshes. Coyote heard them all.

9   But after the stars had closed their eyes, he became very sleepy. His eyelids grew heavy.

10   "I will have to prop my eyes open."

11   So he took two small sticks and propped his eyelids apart. "Now I can stay awake."

12   But soon he was fast asleep. When he awoke, the sun was making shadows. His eyes were dry from being propped open, but he ran to the lodge of the Spirit Chief.

13   "I want to be Grizzly Bear," he said, thinking he was the first one there. The lodge was empty except for Spirit Chief.

14   "That name is taken. Grizzly Bear has the longest arrow. He will be chief of the animals on the earth."

15   "Then I will be Eagle."

16   "That name is taken. Eagle has the second arrow. Eagle will be the chief of the birds."

17   "Then I will be Salmon."

18   "That name is taken. Salmon has the third arrow. Salmon will be the chief of all the fish. Only the shortest arrow is left, and only one name—Coyote."

122

19   And the Spirit Chief gave Coyote the shortest arrow. Coyote sank down beside the fire of the Spirit Chief. His eyes were still dry. The Spirit Chief felt sorry and put water in his eyes. Then Coyote had an idea.

20   "I will ask Grizzly Bear to change with me."

21   "No," said Grizzly, "I cannot. Spirit Chief gave my name to me."

22   Coyote came back and sank down again beside the fire in the big lodge. Then Spirit Chief spoke to him.

23   "I have special power for you. I wanted you to be the last one to come. I have work for you to do. You will need this special power. With it you can change yourself into any form. When you need help, call on your power. Fox will be your brother. He will help you when you need help. If you die, he will have the power to bring you to life again." So that is how Coyote got his special power.

1   **Which animal got the shortest arrow?**

   A Grizzly Bear
   B Eagle
   C Coyote
   D Salmon

2   **Here is a list of names from the passage.**

Coyote	Frog	Salmon	Eagle

   If these names were in alphabetical order, which one would come SECOND?

   F Coyote
   G Frog
   H Salmon
   J Eagle

3 How did Coyote feel about the name he was given?

    A surprised
    B upset
    C pleased
    D angry

4 What will Coyote MOST likely do next?

    F change his name
    G choose a longer stick
    H talk to Grizzly Bear
    J use his special power

5 How did Coyote change in the story? Use details from the story to explain your answer.

_____

_____

_____

_____

_____

_____

_____

_____

_____

_____

THE PRINCESS AND THE PEA

by Hans Christian Andersen (1805–1875)

1   Once upon a time there was a prince who wanted to marry a princess; but she would have to be a real princess. He travelled all over the world to find one, but nowhere could he get what he wanted. There were princesses enough, but it was difficult to find out whether they were real ones. There was always something about them that was not as it should be. So he came home again and was sad, for he would have liked very much to have a real princess.

2   One evening a terrible storm came on; there was thunder and lightning, and the rain poured down in torrents. Suddenly a knocking was heard at the city gate, and the old king went to open it.

3   It was a princess standing out there in front of the gate. But, good gracious! what a sight the rain and the wind had made her look. The water ran down from her hair and clothes; it ran down into the toes of her shoes and out again at the heels. And yet she said that she was a real princess.

4   "Well, we'll soon find that out," thought the old queen. But she said nothing, went into the bed-room, took all the bedding off the bedstead, and laid a pea on the bottom; then she took twenty mattresses and laid them on the pea, and then twenty eider-down beds on top of the mattresses.

5   On this the princess had to lie all night. In the morning she was asked how she had slept.

6   "Oh, very badly!" said she. "I have scarcely closed my eyes all night. Heaven only knows what was in the bed, but I was lying on something hard, so that I am black and blue all over my body. It's horrible!"

7   Now they knew that she was a real princess because she had felt the pea right through the twenty mattresses and the twenty eider-down beds.

8   Nobody but a real princess could be as sensitive as that.

9   So the prince took her for his wife, for now he knew that he had a real princess; and the pea was put in the museum, where it may still be seen, if no one has stolen it.

10   There, that is a true story.

1 **Why didn't the queen think that the girl was a real princess?**

   A She had no crown.
   B She was very old.
   C She wasn't nice.
   D She was very wet.

2 **Look at this picture.**

Which word from the story begins with the same sound?

   F down
   G took
   H black
   J real

3   **What kind of person do you think the queen was? Use details from the passage to support your answer.**

_____

_____

_____

_____

_____

_____

_____

_____

_____

_____

_____

_____

_____

_____

127

THE LOON
by Chief Lalooska

The American Indians in the Pacific Northwest traveled mainly by water because the forests were so thick that it was difficult to travel by land. This story tells how they were able to find their way back to shore.

1   One day, a little girl went deep into the forest. She walked until she found a family of loons. She stopped and played with the loons. In fact, she stayed for several days, becoming good friends with the loons. They taught her many things. But soon, she knew it was time to return to her family, so she said good-bye and returned to her village.

2   In time, this little girl grew to be a Mother and then a Grandmother. One day she was out in a canoe with her two Grandchildren. All of a sudden, the fog rolled in. They couldn't see the shore. They heard a splashing off in the distance. The children thought it was a sea monster. But the Grandmother knew it was something far worse. It was hunters from a tribe farther north. If they captured them, they would take them as slaves. The children would never see their family or village again.

3   The Grandmother told the children to get down in the canoe and be quiet. The other canoe passed by them without seeing them. The children were still hiding in the bottom of the canoe. But how would they find their way back to the village? How would they avoid the hunters in the other canoe?

4   The Grandmother started to sing. The Grandmother sung often. The children thought they knew all of her songs. This was a strange song. The children looked up. Where their Grandmother had been sitting, there was a giant loon. It spread its wings and flew out of the canoe. It circled the canoe and then flew off. The children watched it fly off into the fog. Soon, the loon returned and circled again. When it left this time, the children followed it. It led them safely back to their village. For you see, only the loon has eyes that can see though the fog.

5   When the Grandmother was a girl, playing with the loons, they taught her a song. If she ever sang that song, she would change into a loon FOREVER. So when the American Indians are canoeing in the fog, they always listen for Grandmother loon to guide them back to shore.

128

1   **The grandmother sang the loon song because she wanted –**

    A to catch a loon for herself
    B to save her grandchildren
    C to scare the hunters away
    D to get back to her village

2   **What did the children hear splashing in the fog?**

    F monsters
    G loons
    H Grandmother
    J hunters

3   **Explain what Grandmother did for her grandchildren.**

4   **According to the story, how do American Indians canoeing in the fog find their way home?**

_____

_____

_____

_____

_____

_____

_____

_____

_____

_____

_____

_____

"THE WOLF AND THE STORK"

1   The wolves are prone to play the <u>glutton</u>.

2   One, at a certain feast, 'tis said,

3   So stuffed himself with lamb and mutton,

4   He seemed but little short of dead.

5   Deep in his throat a bone stuck fast.

6   Well for this wolf, who could not speak,

7   That soon a stork quite near him passed.

8   By signs invited, with her beak

9   The bone she drew

10   With slight ado,

11   And for this skillful surgery

12   Demanded, modestly, her fee.

13   "Your fee!" replied the wolf,

14   In accents rather gruff;

15   "And is it not enough

16   Your neck is safe from such a gulf?

17   Go, for a wretch ingrate,

18   Nor tempt again your fate!"

1 What will MOST likely happen the next time the wolf is in trouble?

A The stork will stop and help.

B The stork will pass him by.

C The stork will charge him a fee.

D The stork will sing him a song.

2 In line 1, what does the word <u>glutton</u> mean?

F someone who eats a lot

G someone who shares things

H someone who sings songs

J someone who takes pictures

131

3 **Why did the stork MOST likely stop for the wolf?**

    A The stork and the wolf were best friends.
    B The wolf had helped the stork many times.
    C The stork thought they could help each other.
    D The wolf grabbed the stork as he flew over.

4 **How did the wolf feel about the stork?**

    F He thought the stork was smart.
    G He thought the stork was nice.
    H He thought the stork was bold.
    J He thought the stork was mean.

5 **Was the stork wise to try to help the wolf? Why or why not?**

THE STORY OF THE THREE LITTLE PIGS

by Joseph Jacobs

1   There was once an old sow with three little pigs, and as she had not enough to keep them, she sent them out to seek their fortune. The first that went off met a man with a bundle of straw, and said to him:

2   "Please, man, give me that straw to build me a house."

3   Which the man did, and the little pig built a house with it. Presently came along a wolf, and knocked at the door, and said:

4   "Little pig, little pig, let me come in."

5   To which the pig answered:

6   "No, no, by the hair of my chinny chin chin."

7   The wolf then answered to that:

8   "Then I'll huff, and I'll puff, and I'll blow your house in."

9   So he huffed, and he puffed, and he blew his house in, and ate up the little pig.

10   The second little pig met a man with a pile of wood, and said:

11   "Please, man, give me that wood to build a house."

12   Which the man did, and the pig built his house. Then along came the wolf, and said:

13   "Little pig, little pig, let me come in."

14   "No, no, by the hair of my chinny chin chin."

15   "Then I'll huff, and I'll puff, and I'll blow your house in."

16   So he huffed, and he puffed, and he puffed, and he huffed, and at last he blew the house in, and he ate up the little pig.

17   The third little pig met a man with a load of bricks, and said:

18   "Please, man, give me those bricks to build a house with."

19   So the man gave him the bricks, and he built his house with them. So the wolf came, as he did to the other little pigs, and said:

20   "Little pig, little pig, let me come in."

21   "No, no, by the hair of my chinny chin chin."

22   "Then I'll huff, and I'll puff, and I'll blow your house in."

23   Well, he huffed, and he puffed, and he huffed, and he puffed, and he puffed and huffed; but he could not get the house down.

133

1 **Why did the three little pigs go out on their own?**

A They were excited to be free.

B They could no longer stay home.

C They wanted homes of their own.

D They did not like each other.

2 **The third little pig can BEST be described as –**

F lucky

G brave

H scared

J kind

3 **Which of these happened last in the story?**

A One pig built a house of bricks.

B A man sold a pig some straw.

C One pig built his house with wood.

D A sow let her three pigs go out.

4 **Which part of the story shows that it is make-believe?**

F A house is built out of wood.

G A straw house is knocked down.

H A brick house is made by a pig.

J A wolf cannot blow down a house.

OUCH – THAT HURTS!

1 Did you ever think of pain as being important? Well, it is! Without pain we would not know when and where we hurt.

2 We can tell when we have pain because of nerves. Nerves carry messages to our brain. This, in turn, tells us where we are <u>injured</u>. When we are hurt, we are able to take care of it. A cut, too much heat, or too much cold are bad for our bodies. When we feel pain, it tells us where to take care of our bodies.

3 We may have to fix a cut or get away from something that is too hot. If we are cold, we have to put on warm clothes. Next time you feel pain, think of it as something good for your body!

1 Read this sentence from the passage.

> Without **pain** we would not know when and where we hurt.

Which one of these sounds the same as the underlined word?

A pan
B pail
C pane
D pair

2 This passage is mostly about –

F how to stay warm
G how to help pain
H why we feel pain
J why cuts can hurt

3 Why is pain important?

A It tells us when we are cold.
B It tells us when we are hurt.
C It tells us when we are hot.
D It tells us when we are tired.

4   **What tells our brains when we are hurt?**

   F   nerves
   G   cuts
   H   heat
   J   mouths

136

WHAT'S IN A HAT?

1   Did you know that a hat can tell you a lot about someone? A hat provides warmth, shade, and <u>protection</u> from the weather. We know that. A hat may show the type of job a person has. An example of this would be a tall white hat. This would tell you that the person wearing it is a cook. A navy blue cap with a brim might be part of a police officer's uniform.

2   Hats worn by cowboys were called ten-gallon hats. This is because the wide brims caught the rain. The cowboy then used the full brim to give his horse a drink.

3   Hats may also indicate a person's social status and whether the wearer is wealthy or poor. At one time, beaver hats worn by men and lace hats worn by women were signs of wealth.

1 Why did cowboys wear such big hats?

    A to keep the sun out of their eyes
    B to catch water for their horses
    C to help keep their heads warm
    D to show that they had money

2 What kind of hats do cooks wear?

    F blue hats
    G beaver hats
    H white hats
    J lace hats

3 In paragraph 1, what does the word <u>protection</u> mean?

    A safety
    B heat
    C quiet
    D hope

CARLOS AND JENNY – Part IV

1   Carlos looked worried. "You know, I really want to tell my friends about this cave. But if I do . . . "

2   "Yeah. I wonder about that, too," Jenny admitted.

3   "I don't want people to come here and ruin the cave. I mean, what would we have done without the bat? We might have gotten lost, or made a mess, or accidentally broken the soda straws."

4   Bat settled on a stalactite overhead. *There's one solution. Find a caver group at home. Join up and learn how to be a caver. Then you'll do it right. And you can tell people about this cave if they know how to do it right. I learn a lot from cavers.*

5   Bat then ordered the children to turn off the flashlight.

6   *Lights out, heads down. Go to your left, one last tunnel.*

7   Whispering goodbye to the mysterious handprints, Jenny led the way into the tunnel on her hands and knees. This time the tunnel twisted and turned, taking the occasional hump or valley. Now and then they could hear the bat bump into the wall around sharp corners. Many other tunnels branched off.

8   Without the bat's squeaky <u>instructions</u>, the children knew they would never get back to camp—or find their way back in. Jenny almost believed that Bat was taking them into this tunnel so that they'd never find their way back.

9   At last, Jenny spotted a glimmer of light shining on the tunnel wall.

10   "We're almost out, Carlos!" she shouted.

11   Bat squeaked with excitement. *It's mosquito time! Mosquito time! Sun's down, bugs up, and bats bite!*

12   At last they stood at the cave entrance. Carlos wondered just how many openings there were. The rain had stopped and the sky had darkened as the sun began to set. The cave entrance was hidden behind tall bushes. The camp was at the bottom of the hill. Nobody could see Jenny and Carlos because of the bushes. Campers below were lining up at the dining hall for supper.

13   Jenny looked up at Bat, hanging from a rock. "Thanks for saving us, Bat. Carlos and I will keep your secret. We'll just tell people that we got lost and fell asleep under a big rock. I hope they haven't worried too much."

14   "And we'll come back some day with a cavers' group. We'll be too big to get in that last tunnel," Carlos added.

15   *Thanks kids. Now get yourself back to camp. I'll fly over your campfire tonight. Look for me.*

138

16   With that, the children pushed their way through the bushes and ran down the hill to camp. Behind them, Bat began to zoom through the cloud of bugs that hang around cave entrances. He couldn't remember when he'd been this hungry.

17   Later that night, Carlos and Jenny sat with the other campers around the campfire. While everyone else was slapping mosquitoes, the two friends stared into the night sky. The afternoon's adventure seemed too fantastic to be real. Still, they wondered which of the bats, swooping like great black butterflies overhead, was their Bat.

18   They worried a bit. Had Bat used too much energy in helping them? Did he catch enough mosquitoes? Was he OK after helping them?

19   Just then they heard a familiar squeak just behind their heads. Soft leather wings brushed past their cheeks.

20   *Goodnight, Jenny! Goodnight, Carlos!*

21   The two friends smiled at each other.

22   " 'Night, Bat."

1   What problem did Carlos and Jenny have in the beginning of the story?

  A   They couldn't find Bat.
  B   They were lost in a cave.
  C   They were very hungry.
  D   They couldn't see in the dark.

2   Which one of these questions does paragraph 14 answer?

  F   How can people take care of caves?
  G   Will the children ever visit Bat again?
  H   What makes cavers' groups special?
  J   How big are the children now?

3 Look at this picture.

Which word from the passage begins with the same sound?

A campers
B tunnel
C squeak
D dining

4 **What did Carlos think about telling his friends about the cave?**

F He wanted to keep the cave a secret all to himself.
G He thought his friends would not like the cave at all.
H He was afraid his friends would get lost in the cave.
J He was worried his friends would wreck the cave.

5 **At the end of the story, the children were worried about Bat because –**

A they thought that he was too cold outside in the rain
B they thought that he was too tired from helping them
C they don't think that he can see in the dark
D they don't think he got back to his home

140

6 **What does the word <u>instructions</u> mean in paragraph 8 of this story?**

   F flying

   G rules

   H stories

   J questions

7 **Do you think that the bat in this story was scary? Why or why not?**

ECHO

1   One evening, Mother Bat had to go out and find insects without Echo.

2   "You have grown too big for me to carry," said Mother Bat. "Stay here with the other bat pups. I will be home soon."

3   "Oh, Mother," cried Echo, "I want to fly, too. When can I learn?"

4   "Soon enough," replied Mother Bat.

5   Before she left, Mother Bat warned Echo and the other pups, "Be careful not to fall because there are owls and snakes who would like to have you for their dinner!"

6   Echo and the other bats held on tight to the inside of the tree. They were very scared of the owls and snakes they had heard about.

7   They huddled close together to stay warm and began calling for their mothers.

8   "There she is!" cried Echo. The mother bats returned and greeted their pups.

9   Echo called to his mother, "Over here!" But she flew over to another bat pup.

10 "Mother, over here!" cried Echo again. But Mother Bat flew to another bat pup sniffing and licking its fur. "Oh, why doesn't she hear me?" Echo thought to himself.

11 Finally Mother Bat flew to Echo and started licking his fur. "Why didn't you hear me?" Echo asked his mother.

12 "Well, Echo," replied Mother Bat, "since it is so dark in our hollow tree and there are so many pups, I have to use another sense to find you."

13 "I can tell that you are my baby because of your scent. So, you see, Echo, I had to get close enough to the bat pups to smell their scents."

14 "Bats," continued Mother Bat, "have many different senses and one very special sense that you will learn about later.

15 Echo was very happy that his mother returned. He wondered what other sense his mother was talking about.

16 Echo was a month old and had grown almost as big as his mother.

17 "It is now time for you to learn to fly," said Echo's mother. Echo was so excited. He let go of the tree and began to flap his wings.

18 He fell. He flapped and flapped, but he was still falling. Then slowly, he started to fly. Up and up he went.

19 "Look at me," shouted Echo. "Look at me, Mother, I'm flying!"

1   **Read this sentence from the story.**

> **Echo was very happy that his mother returned.**

   Which word has the same sound as the underlined part of returned?

   A learn
   B cave
   C tune
   D broom

2   **The bats have to be careful not to fall out of their tree so that –**

   F they do not blow away in the wind
   G Mother Bat can find them
   H Echo can talk with the others
   J owls and snakes do not get them

3   **How was Mother Bat able to find Echo?**

   A She felt him.
   B She smelled him.
   C She heard him.
   D She saw him.

4   **Which BEST describes how Echo felt at the end of the story?**

   F afraid
   G tired
   H proud
   J bored

from "THE RAILWAY CHILDREN" – Part II
by Edith Nesbit

1   With the petticoats rolled up under their arms, they ran along the railway, skirting the newly fallen mound of stones and rock and earth, and bent, crushed, twisted trees. They ran at their best pace. Peter led, but the girls were not far behind. They reached the corner that hid the mound from the straight line of railway that ran half a mile without curve or corner.

2   "Now," said Peter, taking hold of the largest flannel petticoat.

3   "You're not"—Phyllis faltered—"you're not going to tear them?"

4   "Shut up," said Peter, with brief sternness.

5   "Oh, yes," said Bobbie, "tear them into little bits if you like. Don't you see, Phil, if we can't stop the train, there'll be a real live accident, with people killed. Oh, horrible! Here, Peter, you'll never tear it through the band!"

6   She took the red flannel petticoat from him and tore it off an inch from the band. Then she tore the other in the same way.

7   "There!" said Peter, tearing in his turn. He divided each petticoat into three pieces. "Now, we've got six flags." He looked at the watch again. "And we've got seven minutes. We must have flagstaffs."

8   The knives given to boys are, for some odd reason, seldom of the kind of steel that keeps sharp. The young saplings had to be broken off. Two came up by the roots. The leaves were stripped from them.

9   "We must cut holes in the flags, and run the sticks through the holes," said Peter. And the holes were cut. The knife was sharp enough to cut flannel with. Two of the flags were set up in <u>heaps</u> of loose stones between the sleepers of the down line. Then Phyllis and Roberta took each a flag, and stood ready to wave it as soon as the train came in sight.

10   "I shall have the other two myself," said Peter, "because it was my idea to wave something red."

11   "They're our petticoats, though," Phyllis was beginning, but Bobbie interrupted—

12   "Oh, what does it matter who waves what, if we can only save the train?"

13   Perhaps Peter had not rightly calculated the number of minutes it would take the 11:29 to get from the station to the place where they were, or perhaps the train was late. Anyway, it seemed a very long time that they waited.

14   Phyllis grew impatient. "I expect the watch is wrong, and the train's gone by," said she.

   144

15   Peter relaxed the heroic attitude he had chosen to show off his two flags. And Bobbie began to feel sick with suspense.

16   It seemed to her that they had been standing there for hours and hours, holding those silly little red flannel flags that no one would ever notice. The train wouldn't care. It would go rushing by them and tear round the corner and go crashing into that awful mound. And everyone would be killed. Her hands grew very cold and trembled so that she could hardly hold the flag. And then came the distant rumble and hum of the metals, and a puff of white steam showed far away along the stretch of line.

1   This story is mostly about –

A   children who try to stop a train
B   a boy who makes flags
C   children who walk along a railway
D   girls who wear petticoats

2   What was Phyllis's main problem in the story?

F   She did not want to listen to Peter.
G   She did not want to wave a flag.
H   She did not want to wait long.
J   She did not want her petticoat torn.

3   In paragraph 9, what does the word <u>heaps</u> mean?

A   bags
B   parts
C   tops
D   piles

4 **Bobbie was most afraid that –**

    F her petticoat would be torn
    G there would be an accident
    H the children would be hurt
    J the train would be late

5 **What happened just after Peter cut the petticoat into flags?**

    A He hooked the flags on sticks.
    B The children waved the flags.
    C The children saw the train.
    D He looked at his watch again.

6 **Read this sentence from the story.**

> **She took the red flannel petticoat from him and tore it off an inch from the band.**

    Which word in this sentence tells what someone did?

    F petticoat
    G tore
    H from
    J inch

    146

7 **What will probably happen next in the story? Use details from the story to explain your answer.**

_____

_____

_____

_____

_____

_____

_____

_____

_____

_____

_____

_____

_____

_____

_____

_____

_____

147

from "THE RAILWAY CHILDREN" – Part III
by Edith Nesbit

1   "Stand firm," said Peter, "and wave like mad! When it gets to that big bush step back, but go on waving! Don't stand on the line, Bobbie!"

2   The train came rattling along very, very fast.

3   "They don't see us! They won't see us! It's all no good!" cried Bobbie.

4   The two little flags on the line <u>swayed</u> as the nearing train shook and loosened the heaps of loose stones that held them up. One of them slowly leaned over and fell on the line. Bobbie jumped forward and caught it up, and waved it; her hands did not tremble now.

5   It seemed that the train came on as fast as ever. It was very near now.

6   "Keep off the line, you silly cuckoo!" said Peter, fiercely.

7   "It's no good," Bobbie said again.

8   "Stand back!" cried Peter, suddenly, and he dragged Phyllis back by the arm.

9   But Bobbie cried, "Not yet, not yet!" and waved her two flags right over the line. The front of the engine looked black and enormous. Its voice was loud and harsh.

10 "Oh, stop, stop, stop!" cried Bobbie. No one heard her. At least Peter and Phyllis didn't, for the oncoming rush of the train covered the sound of her voice with a mountain of sound. But afterwards she used to wonder whether the engine itself had not heard her. It seemed almost as though it had—for it slackened swiftly, slackened and stopped, not twenty yards from the place where Bobbie's two flags waved over the line. She saw the great black engine stop dead, but somehow she could not stop waving the flags. And when the driver and the fireman had got off the engine and Peter and Phyllis had gone to meet them and pour out their excited tale of the awful mound just round the corner, Bobbie still waved the flags.

11 When the station was reached, the three were the heroes.

12 The praises they got for their "prompt action," their "common sense," their "ingenuity," were enough to have turned anybody's head. Phyllis enjoyed herself thoroughly. She had never been a real heroine before, and the feeling was delicious. Peter's ears got very red. Yet he, too, enjoyed himself. Only Bobbie wished they all wouldn't. She wanted to get away.

13 "You'll hear from the Company about this, I expect," said the Station Master.

14 Bobbie wished she might never hear of it again. She pulled at Peter's jacket.

15 "Oh, come away, come away! I want to go home," she said.

148

16   So they went. And as they went the Station Master and Porter and guards and driver and fireman and passengers sent up a cheer.

17   "Oh, listen," cried Phyllis; "that's for us!"

18   "Yes," said Peter. "I say, I am glad I thought about something red, and waving it."

19   "How lucky we did put on our red flannel petticoats!" said Phyllis.

20   Bobbie said nothing. She was thinking of the horrible mound, and the trustful train rushing towards it.

21   "And it was us that saved them," said Peter.

1   What is the theme of this story?

   A   Children should listen to grown-ups.
   B   Things aren't always as they seem.
   C   Children can make a difference.
   D   Friends should help each other.

2   In paragraph 4, what does the word <u>swayed</u> mean?

   F   rocked back and forth
   G   shined brightly
   H   fell to the ground
   J   bent in half

3   Bobbie can BEST be described as –

   A   excited
   B   quiet
   C   careful
   D   hopeful

149

4 **In a short paragraph, summarize the story.**

_____

_____

_____

_____

_____

_____

_____

_____

_____

_____

_____

_____

_____

_____

_____

_____

from "THE PRINCESS AND THE GOBLIN"
Part II
by George MacDonald

CHAPTER 4: What the Nurse Thought of It

1   "Why, where can you have been, princess?" asked the nurse, taking her in her arms. "It's very unkind of you to hide away so long. I began to be afraid—" Here she checked herself.

2   "What were you afraid of, nursie?" asked the princess.

3   "Never mind," she answered. "Perhaps I will tell you another day. Now tell me where you have been."

4   "I've been up a long way to see my very great, huge, old grandmother," said the princess.

5   "What do you mean by that?" asked the nurse, who thought she was making fun.

6   "I mean that I've been a long way up and up to see My GREAT grandmother. Ah, nursie, you don't know what a beautiful mother of grandmothers I've got upstairs. She is such an old lady, with such lovely white hair—as white as my silver cup. Now, when I think of it, I think her hair must be silver."

7   "What nonsense you are talking, princess!" said the nurse.

8   "I'm not talking <u>nonsense</u>," returned Irene, rather offended. "I will tell you all about her. She's much taller than you, and much prettier."

9   "Oh, I dare say!" remarked the nurse.

10   "And she lives upon pigeons' eggs."

11   "Most likely," said the nurse.

12   "And she sits in an empty room, spin-spinning all day long."

13   "Not a doubt of it," said the nurse.

14   "And she keeps her crown in her bedroom."

15   "Of course—quite the proper place to keep her crown in. She wears it in bed, I'll be bound."

16   "She didn't say that. And I don't think she does. That wouldn't be comfortable—would it? I don't think my papa wears his crown for a night-cap. Does he, nursie?"

17   "I never asked him. I dare say he does."

18   "And she's been there ever since I came here—ever so many years."

19   "Anybody could have told you that," said the nurse, who did not believe a word Irene was saying.

20   "Why didn't you tell me, then?"

21   "There was no necessity. You could make it all up for yourself."

22   "You don't believe me, then!" exclaimed the princess, astonished and angry, as she well might be.

23   "Did you expect me to believe you, princess?" asked the nurse coldly. "I know princesses are in the habit of telling make-believes, but you are the first I ever heard of who expected to have them believed," she added, seeing that the child was strangely in earnest.

24   The princess burst into tears.

25   "Well, I must say," remarked the nurse, now thoroughly vexed with her for crying, "it is not at all becoming in a princess to tell stories and expect to be believed just because she is a princess."

26   "But it's quite true, I tell you."

27   "You've dreamt it, then, child."

28   "No, I didn't dream it. I went upstairs, and I lost myself, and if I hadn't found the beautiful lady, I should never have found myself."

29   "Oh, I dare say!"

30   "Well, you just come up with me, and see if I'm not telling the truth."

31   "Indeed I have other work to do. It's your dinnertime, and I won't have any more such nonsense."

1   **Which word BEST describes how the princess felt when Nursie didn't believe her story?**

   A   angry
   B   excited
   C   happy
   D   scared

2 In paragraph 8, what does the word <u>nonsense</u> mean?

    F happiness
    G games
    H jokes
    J silliness

3 What will Nursie MOST likely do next?

    A make dinner for the princess
    B go upstairs to see the grandmother
    C give the princess a crown
    D talk with the princess some more

4 Read this sentence about the story.

> The nurse did not _____ that the princess's _____ _____ was true!

  Which words make the sentence correct?

    F no, hole, tail
    G know, whole, tale
    H no, whole, tail
    J know, hole, tale

5 This story is mostly about –

    A a princess who has seen someone that no one else has seen
    B a princess who is scared by the stories that her nurse tells her
    C a princess who makes up stories about her grandmother
    D a princess who enjoys sneaking away to make her nurse worry

153

6 **Would you believe the princess? Why or why not? Use details from the passage to support your answer.**

_____

_____

_____

_____

_____

_____

_____

_____

_____

_____

_____

_____

_____

_____

_____

WHY PORCUPINE HAS QUILLS

1   Once, long ago, Porcupine had feathers. The people didn't know whether Porcupine was a bird or a mammal. Porcupine liked to boast about this.

2   Duck hated boasting. In those days, everybody hated all sorts of bragging. Especially the Great Spirit.

3   "Oh Honorable Spirit. Oh, one of great power. I come from the North to ask of you a favor," Duck said, bowing low when he came to the home of the Great Spirit.

4   "Surely it is not you, Duck; you have always been loyal to your gods, spirits, and beliefs. Why have you come?" the Great Spirit boomed with much concern in his voice.

5   "Porcupine has been boasting." Duck paused, searching for the next word.

6   Before he could get it out, the Great Spirit interrupted him. "Of course. Of course. I should have known that Porcupine needed some discipline! You best be on your way now. Good-bye, Duck," he said.

7   "I really should not have given Porcupine feathers. I should have known something like this would happen!" the Great Spirit muttered to himself, thinking of a plan.

8   "So now, fellow bird, I have a surprise for you. Tonight I shall go into the village and steal fire from the humans. Your friends dared me to do so." Porcupine grinned in delight as Duck's face lit up with excitement.

9   "But oh, Porcupine, how shall you bring the fire back?" Duck had realized that problem immediately, but Porcupine wasn't too bright.

10   "Why, I'll carry it on my back, of course!" Porcupine answered. Duck didn't tell him that fire could burn feathers. Duck didn't tell Porcupine because she felt that was what the Great Spirit wanted her to do.

11   And so the night fell. Porcupine set off to the village. Duck and her friends looked for a last glimpse of him, because they all knew that would be the last time they saw him with feathers.

12   Late into the night, Porcupine came back. The fire had burned out on his back. All there was left were a few burnt quills. Porcupine didn't notice until his friends pointed it out. He was angry, but he didn't have anything else left to brag about.

13   And to this day, Porcupine has quills.

1   **What is the theme of this story?**

   A   A bird is a pretty thing.
   B   It's not nice to brag.
   C   Stay away from fire.
   D   Don't listen to a duck.

2   **Compared to Porcupine, Duck was –**

   F   less boastful
   G   more friendly
   H   less truthful
   J   more foolish

3   **The Great Spirit can BEST be described as –**

   A   happy
   B   nice
   C   tricky
   D   afraid

4 **Why do you think that the Great Spirit wanted Porcupine to have only quills and no feathers? Use details from the story to support your answer.**

_____

_____

_____

_____

_____

_____

_____

_____

_____

_____

_____

_____

_____

_____

_____

_____

_____

"LITTLE BOY BLUE"

by Eugene Field (1850–1895)

1   The little toy dog is covered with dust,
2   But sturdy and stanch he stands;
3   And the little toy soldier is red with rust,
4   And his musket moulds in his hands.
5   Time was when the little toy dog was new,
6   And the soldier was passing fair;
7   And that was the time when our Little Boy Blue
8   Kissed them and put them there.
9   "Now, don't you go till I come," he said,
10   "And don't you make any noise!"
11   So, toddling off to his trundle-bed,
12   He dreamt of the pretty toys;
13   And, as he was dreaming, an angel song
14   Awakened our Little Boy Blue—
15   Oh! the years are many, the years are long,
16   But the little toy friends are true!
17   Ay, faithful to Little Boy Blue they stand,
18   Each in the same old place—
19   Awaiting the touch of a little hand,
20   The smile of a little face;
21   And they wonder, as waiting the long years through
22   In the dust of that little chair,
23   What has become of our Little Boy Blue,
24   Since he kissed them and put them there.

1 Read this line from the poem.

> **What has become of our Little <u>Boy</u> Blue . . .**

Which word rhymes with <u>boy</u>?

A buoy
B toy
C dog
D true

2 How many syllables are in the word "smile"?

    F 1
    G 2
    H 3
    J 4

3 What do the toys hope will happen?

    A Little Boy Blue will put them away.
    B Little Boy Blue will dust them off.
    C Little Boy Blue will play with them.
    D Little Boy Blue will find friends for them.

159

THE WOLF AND THE PIG

1   Finding that he could not, with all his huffing and puffing, blow the pig's brick house down, the wolf said, "Little pig, I know where there is a nice field of turnips."

2   "Where?" said the little pig.

3   "Oh, in Mr. Smith's field. If you will be ready tomorrow morning, we will go together and get some for dinner."

4   "Very well," said the little pig. "What time do you mean to go?"

5   "Oh, at six o'clock."

6   So the little pig got up at five o'clock and got the turnips before the wolf came crying, "Little pig, are you ready?"

7   The little pig said, "Ready! I have been and come back again, and got a nice potful for dinner."

8   The wolf felt very angry when he heard this, but thought that he would be a match for the little pig somehow or other, so he said, "Little pig, I know where there is a nice apple tree."

9   "Where?" asked the pig.

10   "Down at Merry-garden," replied the wolf. "If you will not deceive me, I will come for you at five o'clock tomorrow. We can get some apples."

11   The little pig got up next morning at four o'clock. He went off for the apples. He hoped to get back before the wolf came, but it took a long time to climb the tree.

160

12   Just as he was coming down from it, he saw the wolf coming. When the wolf came up he said, "Little pig, what! are you here before me? Are they nice apples?"

13   "Yes, very," said the little pig. "I will throw you down one."

14   And he threw it far. While the wolf went to pick it up, the little pig jumped down and ran home.

15   The next day the wolf came again and said to the little pig, "Little pig, there is a fair in town this afternoon; will you go?"

16   "Oh yes," said the pig, "I will go; what time?"

17   "At three o'clock," said the wolf.

18   As usual, the little pig went off beforehand. He got to the fair and bought a butter churn. He was rolling it home when he saw the wolf coming. He got into the churn to hide. In so doing, he knocked it over. It rolled down the hill with the pig in it. That frightened the wolf so much that he ran home without going to the fair. He went to the little pig's house. The wolf told the pig how frightened he had been by a great round thing that came past him down the hill. Then the little pig said, "Ha! ha! I frightened you then!"

19   Then the wolf was very angry indeed. He tried to get down the chimney in order to eat up the little pig. When the little pig saw what he was about, he put a pot full of water on the blazing fire. Just as the wolf was coming down, he took off the cover. In fell the wolf. Quickly, the little pig clapped on the cover. When the wolf was boiled, the pig ate him for supper.

161

1   **What happened just after the wolf found the little pig in the apple tree?**

   A   The wolf tried to go down the chimney.
   B   The little pig threw an apple from the tree.
   C   The little pig ran home and got away.
   D   The wolf asked the pig to go to Mr. Smith's field.

2   **In paragraph 10, what does the word <u>deceive</u> mean?**

   F   trick
   G   calm
   H   hurt
   J   touch

3   **How did the pig finally get rid of the wolf?**

   A   The pig cooked the wolf in a pot of soup.
   B   The pig rolled the wolf down a big hill.
   C   The pig left the wolf at the fair.
   D   The pig made the wolf chase an apple.

4   **Which list of words from the story is in alphabetical order?**

   F   brick, before, butter, bought
   G   where, what, when, while
   H   tomorrow, turnip, time, together
   J   chimney, churn, cover, crying

5 Do you like how this story ended? Why or why not?

THE GOLDEN RIVER

1   There was once a beautiful little valley where the sun was warm and the rains fell softly. Its apples were so red, its corn so yellow, and its grapes so blue that it was called the Treasure Valley. Not a river ran into it, but one great river flowed down the mountains on the other side. Because the setting sun always tinged its high waterfall with gold after the rest of the world was dark, it was called the Golden River. The lovely valley belonged to two brothers. The younger, little Gluck, was happy-hearted and kind. Hans was cruel and mean. He was hard to his farmhands, hard to his customers, hard to the poor, and hardest of all to Gluck.

2   At last, Hans became so bad that the Spirit of the West Wind took vengeance. He forbade any of the gentle winds—south and west—to bring rain to the valley. Then, since there were no rivers in it, it dried up. Instead of a treasure valley, it became a desert of dry, red sand.

3   Hans went out every day. He did no work. All he did was spend money. He left Gluck in the house to work. At last, the only precious thing left was Gluck's gold mug. Hans decided to melt it into spoons to sell. He ignored Gluck's tears. He put the mug in the melting pot. Then he went out, leaving Gluck to watch it.

4   Poor little Gluck sat at the window. As the sun began to go down, he saw the beautiful waterfall of the Golden River turn red, yellow, and then pure gold.

5   "Oh, dear!" he said to himself. "How fine it would be if the river were really golden! I needn't be poor then."

6   "It wouldn't be fine at all!" said a thin, metallic little voice in his ear.

7   "Mercy, what's that!" said Gluck, looking all about, but nobody was there.

8   Suddenly, the sharp little voice came again. "Pour me out," it said. "I am too hot!"

9   It seemed to come right from the oven. Gluck stood, staring in fright. It came again, "Pour me out; I'm too hot!"

164

10   Gluck was very much frightened, but he went and looked in the melting pot. When he touched it, the little voice said, "Pour me out, I say!" And Gluck took the handle and began to pour the gold out.

11   First, a tiny pair of yellow legs came out. Then came a pair of yellow coattails. Then, a strange little yellow body. Last, a wee yellow face with long curls of gold hair appeared. And the whole put itself together as it fell and stood up on the floor. He was the strangest little yellow man—only about a foot high!

12   "Dear, me!" said Gluck.

13   But the little yellow man said, "Gluck, do you know who I am? I am the King of the Golden River."

14   Gluck did not know what to say, so he said nothing. Indeed, the little man gave him no chance. He said, "Gluck, I have been watching you, and what I have seen of you, I like. Listen, and I will tell you something for your good. Whoever shall climb to the top of the mountain from which the Golden River falls, and shall cast into its waters three drops of holy water, for him and him only shall its waters turn to gold. But no one can succeed except at the first trial. Anyone who casts unholy water in the river will be turned into a black stone."

15   And then, before Gluck could draw his breath, the king walked straight into the hottest flame of the fire and vanished up the chimney!

16   When Gluck's brother came home, Gluck told him about the King of the Golden River. Hans decided to get the gold. The priest would not give such a bad man any holy water, so he stole a bottle. Then, he took a basket of bread and wine. He began to climb the mountain.

17   Hans climbed fast. Soon, he came to the end of the first hill, but there he found a great glacier. It was a hill of ice. He had never seen it before. It was horrible to cross. The ice was slippery. Great gulfs yawned before him. Noises like groans and shrieks came from under his feet. He lost his basket of bread and wine. He grew quite faint with fear and exhaustion. Finally, his feet touched firm ground again.

    165

18   Next, Hans came to a hill of hot, red rock. It had not a bit of grass to ease the feet or a particle of shade. After an hour's climb, he was so thirsty that he felt that he must drink. He looked at the flask of water. "Three drops are enough," he thought. "I will just cool my lips." He was lifting the flask to his lips when he saw something beside him in the path. It was a small dog. It seemed to be dying of thirst. Its tongue was out and its legs were lifeless. A swarm of black ants were crawling about its lips. It looked piteously at the bottle that Hans held. Hans raised the bottle, drank, kicked at the animal, and passed on.

19   A strange black shadow came across the blue sky.

20   Hans climbed for another hour. The rocks grew hotter and the way steeper every moment. At last he could bear it no longer; he must drink. The bottle was half empty, but he decided to drink half of what was left. As he lifted it, something moved in the path beside him. It was a child, lying nearly dead of thirst on the rock. Her eyes were closed. Her lips burned and her breath came in gasps. Hans looked at her, drank, and passed on.

21   A dark cloud came over the sun and long shadows crept up the mountainside.

22   The way grew very steep now. The air weighed like lead on Hans's forehead, but the Golden River was very near. Hans stopped a moment to breathe. Then, he started to climb the last height.

23   As he clambered on, he saw an old, old man lying in the path. His eyes were sunken and his face was deadly pale.

24   "Water!" he said. "Water!"

25   "I have none for you," said Hans. "You have had your share of life." He strode over the old man's body and climbed on.

26   A flash of blue lightning dazzled him for an instant, then the heavens were dark.

27   At last, Hans stood on the brink of the waterfall of the Golden River. The sound of its roaring filled the air. He drew the flask from his side and hurled it into the torrent. As he did so, an icy chill shot through him. He shrieked and fell. The river rose and flowed over the Black Stone.

28   When Hans did not come back, Gluck grieved. Gluck found himself

166

alone. He decided to try his luck with the King of the Golden River. The priest gave him some holy water as soon as he asked for it. With this and a basket of bread, Gluck started off.

29 The hill of ice was much harder for Gluck to climb because he was not so strong as his brother. He lost his bread. He fell often. He was exhausted when he got on firm ground. He began to climb the hill in the hottest part of the day. When he had climbed for an hour, he was very thirsty. He lifted the bottle to drink a little water. As he did so, he saw a feeble old man coming down the path toward him.

30 "I am faint with thirst," said the old man. "Will you give me some of that water?"

31 Gluck saw that he was pale and tired, so he gave him the water, saying, "Please don't drink it all." But the old man drank a great deal. He gave back the bottle two-thirds emptied. Then, he bade Gluck good speed. Gluck went on merrily.

32 Some grass appeared on the path. Grasshoppers began to sing.

33 At the end of another hour, Gluck felt that he must drink again. However, as he raised the flask, he saw a little child lying by the roadside. She cried out pitifully for water. After a struggle with himself, Gluck decided to bear the thirst a little longer. He put the bottle to the child's lips. The child drank all but a few drops. Then, she got up and ran down the hill.

34 All kinds of sweet flowers began to grow on the rocks. Crimson and purple butterflies flitted about in the air.

35 At the end of another hour, Gluck's thirst was almost unbearable. He saw that there were only five or six drops of water in the bottle, however. He did not dare to drink. He was putting the flask away again when he saw a little dog on the rocks, gasping for breath. He remembered the dwarf's words: "No one can succeed except at the first trial."

36 He tried to pass the dog, but it whined piteously. Gluck stopped. He could not bear to pass it.

"Confound the king and his gold, too!" he said. He poured the few drops of water into the dog's mouth.

37   The dog sprang up. Its tail disappeared. Its nose grew red. Its eyes <u>twinkled</u>. The next minute, the dog was gone. The King of the Golden River stood there. He stooped and plucked a lily that grew beside Gluck's feet. Three drops of dew were on its white leaves. These the dwarf shook into the flask that Gluck held in his hand.

38   "Cast these into the river," he said, "and go down the other side of the mountains into the Treasure Valley." Then he disappeared.

39   Gluck stood on the brink of the Golden River. He cast the three drops of dew into the stream. Gluck was disappointed not to see gold, but he obeyed the King of the Golden River. He went down the other side of the mountains.

40   When he came out into the Treasure Valley, a river, like the Golden River, was springing from a new canyon in the rocks above. It was flowing among the heaps of dry sand. Fresh grass sprang beside the river. Flowers opened along the river's sides. Vines began to cover the whole valley. The Treasure Valley was becoming a garden again.

41   Gluck lived in the valley. His grapes were blue. His apples were red. His corn was yellow. The poor were never driven from his door. For him, as the king had promised, the river was really a River of Gold.

1   **When Hans decided to melt Gluck's golden mug, Gluck cried because he –**

   A   didn't like being poor
   B   didn't like working
   C   loved his golden mug
   D   was tired and hungry

2   **What lesson can you learn from this story?**

   F   It is good to help others.
   G   It is important to find gold.
   H   It is better to be strong than kind.
   J   It is better to be poor than smart.

3 Look at this picture.

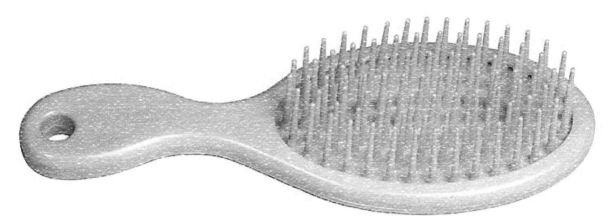

Which word from the story begins with the same sound?

A brother
B mountain
C gold
D river

4 What would MOST likely have happened if Hans had helped the thirsty people and the dog?

F He would have lived in Treasure Valley.
G He would have been given lots of gold.
H He would have gotten to keep the nice dog.
J He would have made Gluck very angry.

5 In paragraph 37, what does the word <u>twinkled</u> mean?

A closed
B watered
C sparkled
D winked

169

6 **What was Hans's main problem in the story?**

    F He did not like Gluck.
    G He was afraid of a spirit.
    H He did not have money.
    J He saw a little gold man.

7 **Hans can BEST be described as –**

    A scared
    B kind
    C nasty
    D weak

8 **Why does the story say that " . . . the river was really a River of Gold" when it was still just water?**

WHY IS THE SKY BLUE?

1   Light is energy that can travel through space. Light looks white, but it is really many colors. The colors in light are red, orange, yellow, green, blue, and violet. When you look at a rainbow in the sky, you see these colors.

2   The sky is filled with tiny gas molecules and small bits of solid stuff, like dust. When light from the sun goes through the air, it hits these things. Different colors in the light act in different ways when they bump into a gas molecule. The blue light goes in all different directions. It makes the whole sky look blue. The red and orange light pass straight through the air.

3   You can do an <u>experiment</u> to see how light travels. It will help you to better understand how to make things work together. You can also learn how light responds to other things around it.

SPLIT LIGHT INTO DIFFERENT COLORS

What you need:

- a big pan
- a mirror that will fit in the pan
- a piece of white paper
- water
- direct sunlight

    171

What to do:

1. Put water in the pan. Don't fill it to the top.

2. Put the pan in the sunlight.

3. Put the mirror under the water in the pan. Make sure it faces the sun.

4. Hold the paper above the water.

5. Move the paper and mirror until the reflected light hits the paper.

6. Observe the colors shown on the paper.

173

1 **To see all the colors of light, you should look at –**

    A clouds
    B water
    C rainbows
    D sunshine

2 **The sky is blue because blue light –**

    F moves faster than other lights
    G goes in different directions
    H is brighter than other lights
    J is much higher in the sky

3 **In paragraph 3, what does the word <u>experiment</u> mean?**

    A game
    B play
    C job
    D test

4 **The author organized the information in the "What to do" part of the passage by –**

    F stating a main idea and giving examples
    G listing what you will need to do something
    H asking a question and then answering it
    J listing the steps needed to do something

from "BLACK BEAUTY"

by Anna Sewell

CHAPTER 1

My Early Home

1   The first place that I can well remember was a large pleasant meadow with a pond of clear water in it. Some shady trees leaned over the pond. Rushes and water-lilies grew at the deep end of the pond. Over the hedge on one side we looked into a plowed field. On the other we looked over a gate at our master's house. It stood by the roadside. At the top of the meadow was a grove of fir trees. At the bottom was a running brook overhung by a steep bank.

2   While I was young I lived upon my mother's milk, as I could not eat grass. In the daytime I ran by her side. At night I lay down close by her. When it was hot we used to stand by the pond in the shade of the trees. When it was cold we had a nice warm shed near the grove.

3   As soon as I was old enough to eat grass my mother used to go out to work in the daytime, and come back in the evening.

4   There were six young colts in the meadow besides me. They were older than I was. Some were nearly as large as grown-up horses. I used to run with them, and had great fun. We used to gallop all together round and round the field as hard as we could go. Sometimes we had rather rough play, for they would frequently bite and kick as well as gallop.

5   One day, when there was a good deal of kicking, my mother whinnied to me to come to her. She said:

6   "I wish you to pay attention to what I am going to say to you. The colts who live here are very good colts, but they are cart-horse colts. Of course they have not learned manners. You have been well-bred and well-born. Your father has a great name in these parts. Your grandfather won the cup two years at the Newmarket races. Your grandmother had the sweetest temper of any horse I ever knew. I think you have never seen me kick or bite. I hope you will grow up gentle and good, and never learn bad ways. Do your work with a good will, lift your feet up well when you trot, and never bite or kick even in play."

7   I have never forgotten my mother's advice. I knew she was a wise old horse, and our master thought a great deal of her. Her name was Duchess, but he often called her Pet.

8   Our master was a good, kind man. He gave us good food, good lodging, and kind words. He spoke as kindly to us as he did to his little children. We were all fond of him. My mother loved him very much. When she saw him at the gate she would neigh with joy, and trot up to him. He would pat and stroke her and say, "Well, old Pet, and how is your little Darkie?" I was a dull black, so he called me Darkie. Then he would give me a piece of bread, which was very good. Sometimes he brought a carrot for my mother. All the horses would come to him, but I think we were his favorites. My mother always took him to the town on a market day in a light gig.

9   There was a plowboy, Dick, who sometimes came into our field to pluck blackberries from the hedge. When he had eaten all he wanted he would have what he called fun with the colts, throwing stones and sticks at them to make them gallop. We did not much mind him, for we could gallop off; but sometimes a stone would hit and hurt us.

10   One day he was at this game, and did not know that the master was in the next field. But he was there, watching what was going on. Over the hedge he jumped in a snap. Catching Dick by the arm, he gave him such a box on the ear as made him roar with the pain and surprise. As soon as we saw the master we trotted up nearer to see what went on.

11   "Bad boy!" he said, "bad boy! to chase the colts. This is not the first time, nor the second, but it shall be the last. There—take your money and go home. I shall not want you on my farm again." So we never saw Dick anymore. Old Daniel, the man who looked after the horses, was just as gentle as our master, so we were well off.

CHAPTER 2

The Hunt

12   Before I was two years old a circumstance happened which I have never forgotten. It was early in the spring. There had been a little frost in the night. A light mist still hung over the woods and meadows. I and the other colts were feeding at the lower part of the field when we heard, quite in the distance,

176

what sounded like the cry of dogs. The oldest of the colts raised his head, pricked his ears, and said, "There are the hounds!"

13 He immediately cantered off, followed by the rest of us to the upper part of the field. From there we could look over the hedge and see several fields beyond. My mother and an old riding horse of our master's were also standing near, and seemed to know all about it.

14 "They have found a hare," said my mother, "and if they come this way we shall see the hunt."

15 And soon the dogs were all tearing down the field of young wheat next to ours. I never heard such a noise as they made. They did not bark, nor howl, nor whine, but kept on a "yo! yo, o, o! yo! yo, o, o!" at the top of their voices. After them came a number of men on horseback. Some of them were in green coats. All were galloping as fast as they could.

16 The old horse snorted and looked eagerly after them. We young colts wanted to be galloping with them, but they were soon away into the fields lower down. Here it seemed as if they had come to a stand. The dogs left off barking, and ran about every way with their noses to the ground.

17 "They have lost the scent," said the old horse. "Perhaps the hare will get off."

18 "What hare?" I said.

19 "Oh! I don't know what hare. Likely enough it may be one of our own hares out of the woods. Any hare they can find will do for the dogs and men to run after."

20 Before long the dogs began their "yo! yo, o, o!" again. Back they came altogether at full speed, making straight for our meadow at the part where the high bank and hedge overhang the brook.

21 "Now we shall see the hare," said my mother. Just then a hare wild with fright rushed by and made for the woods. On came the dogs. They burst over the bank, leaped the stream, and came dashing across the field followed by the huntsmen. Six or eight men leaped their horses clean over, close upon the dogs. The hare tried to get through the fence. It was too thick. She turned sharp round to make for the road, but it was too late. The dogs were upon her with their wild cries. We heard one shriek, and that was the end of her. One

177

of the huntsmen rode up and whipped off the dogs, who would soon have torn her to pieces. He held her up by the leg torn and bleeding. All the gentlemen seemed well pleased.

22   As for me, I was so astonished that I did not at first see what was going on by the brook. When I did look there was a sad sight. Two fine horses were down. One was struggling in the stream. The other was <u>groaning</u> on the grass. One of the riders was getting out of the water covered with mud. The other lay quite still.

23   "His neck is broke," said my mother.

24   "And serve him right, too," said one of the colts.

25   I thought the same, but my mother did not join with us.

26   "Well, no," she said, "you must not say that. But though I am an old horse, and have seen and heard a great deal, I never yet could make out why men are so fond of this sport. They often hurt themselves and spoil good horses. They tear up the fields. It's all for a hare or a fox, or a stag, that they could get more easily some other way. But we are only horses, and don't know."

27   While my mother was saying this we stood and looked on. Many of the riders had gone to the young man; but my master, who had been watching what was going on, was the first to raise him. His head fell back and his arms hung down. Every one looked very serious. There was no noise now. Even the dogs were quiet, and seemed to know that something was wrong. They carried him to our master's house. I heard afterward that it was young George Gordon, the squire's only son, a fine, tall young man, and the pride of his family.

28   Mr. Bond, the farrier, came to look at the black horse that lay groaning on the grass. He felt him all over, and shook his head. One of his legs was broken. Then some one ran to our master's house and came back with a gun. Presently there was a loud bang and a dreadful shriek. Then all was still. The black horse moved no more.

1 Duchess, the speaker's mother, can BEST be described as –

A quiet
B tired
C wise
D playful

2 Read this sentence from the story.

They were old<u>er</u> than I was.

Adding –<u>er</u> to the word old makes a word that means –

F not old
G too old
H more old
J most old

3 Where did the speaker go when it got cold?

A in a shed
B in a house
C to the grove
D to the pond

4 What did Duchess tell the speaker never to do?

F jump and push
G scream and cry
H cry and hide
J kick and bite

5 **Which question does paragraph 6 answer?**

    A What did the speaker's home look like?

    B What kind of man was the speaker's master?

    C How was the speaker different from the other colts?

    D Why were men on horses chasing after the hounds?

6 **In paragraph 22, what does the word <u>groaning</u> mean?**

    F running

    G playing

    H crying

    J lying

180

MAKING VEGETABLE SOUP

1   Vegetables are a very important part of a healthy, balanced diet (unless they are deep fried). When properly prepared, vegetables are low in fat and high in vitamins, minerals, and proteins so necessary for growing children and for adults, too. Sometimes, just the thought of eating vegetables makes some kids very unhappy, but you should know that they are very good for you.

2   One way to make eating vegetables more fun is to get involved in preparing meals with someone else in your household. Cooking can be very interesting. You can learn by watching an adult so one day you can do it for yourself.

3   There is nothing quite as <u>cozy</u> as a warm bowl of vegetable soup on a cold, blustery day. Here is an easy recipe for vegetable soup. Ask an adult to help you to make this delicious treat. It will make you wish you could eat vegetables with every meal!

Ingredients:

- lots of different vegetables (potatoes, onion, peppers, carrots, etc.)
- one teaspoon of salt
- half a cup of cooked rice
- two beef bouillon cubes
- water

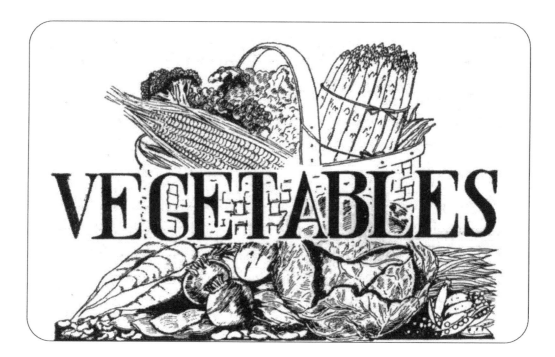

181

Method:

1. Peel the vegetables or remove cores.
2. Wash the vegetables with cold water.
3. Chop the vegetables into bite-size pieces.
4. Place the vegetables into a saucepan.
5. Add the salt and rice.
6. Fill the pot with enough water to cover all the ingredients.
7. Add the beef bouillon cubes.
8. Boil the vegetables for several minutes.
9. Reduce the heat and simmer until the vegetables are cooked.
10. Serve and enjoy!

1 **This passage is mostly about –**

   A why vegetables are fun
   B how to grow vegetables
   C vegetables that taste good
   D making vegetable soup

2 **What is the first thing you should do after gathering the ingredients for your soup?**

   F wash the vegetables
   G chop the vegetables
   H peel the vegetables
   J boil the vegetables

182

3 **It is important to eat vegetables because they –**

    A   are easy to make
    B   taste very good
    C   are good for you
    D   make good soup

4 **Which one of these questions does paragraph 1 answer?**

    F   How can I learn to make vegetable soup?
    G   Why should I eat more vegetables?
    H   How can I make eating vegetables fun?
    J   What do I need to make vegetable soup?

5 **How many syllables are in the word "ingredients"?**

    A   1
    B   2
    C   3
    D   4

6 **In paragraph 3, what does the word <u>cozy</u> mean?**

    F   tasteless
    G   quiet
    H   different
    J   comfortable

7 **What other foods might be tasty in a vegetable soup? Why? Which would not taste so good in soup of any kind? Explain your answer.**

_____

_____

_____

_____

_____

_____

_____

_____

_____

_____

_____

_____

_____

_____

_____

Made in the USA
Lexington, KY
14 April 2015